MANAGING CHANGE
in the NHS

MANAGING CHANGE
in the NHS

TRUDY UPTON
and
BERNARD BROOKS

OPEN UNIVERSITY PRESS
Buckingham • Philadelphia

Open University Press
Celtic Court
22 Ballmoor
Buckingham
MK18 1XW

email: enquiries@openup.co.uk
world wide web: www.openup.co.uk

and
325 Chestnut Street
Philadelphia, PA 19106, USA

First Published 1995
Reprinted 1999, 2000, 2002

A catalogue record for this book is available from the British Library

ISBN   0 335 20593 3 (pbk)

Typeset by JS Typesetting, Wellingborough, Northants.
Printed and bound in Great Britain by Biddles Ltd
www.biddles.co.uk

Contents

Contents

Preface

Since its inception nearly 50 years ago the NHS has been in a process of development. It did not spring fully formed and fixed in 1948 but has been tossed and turned by the vicissitudes of political will and by the rapidly changing social picture experienced throughout its history.

The health service is no stranger to change therefore, but I think it would be acknowledged by all that in the four years since the introduction of the NHS reforms healthcare managers have had to see through one of the biggest revolutions witnessed in any part of the public sector.

The reforms have caused fundamental changes to every aspect of the NHS. The purchaser/provider split has caused its own waves and led on recently to the integration of FHSA and HAs, the merger of trusts and the move to a primary care led service.

What individual managers need at times like this is support and a means of testing their decisions against a well-rehearsed and systematic framework. *Managing Change in the NHS* provides just that. It will be a real benefit for all those attempting to take the opportunities offered by the catalyst of the reforms to bring real improvements to the quality and cost effectiveness of the service we give to patients.

Philip Hunt
Director, NAHAT

NAHAT

NAHAT (National Association of Health Authorities and Trusts) is the leading organization working for NHS management bodies. It brings together NHS authorities, health boards and NHS trusts into one representative organization covering the separate and collective views of both purchasers and providers. It represents members' interests to Ministers and to other decision-makers. It promotes the benefits of the NHS and provides its members with a wide range of support services, research, conferences and publications as an aid to the delivery of high-quality healthcare.

Series Editor's Foreword

'Fitter, leaner organizations' has been the catch-phrase for the process of removing layers of middle managers from NHS organizations. For senior managers this has meant either taking on more work and facing personal burnout or delegating tasks and authority to staff who have not worked as managers in the past and who do not usually feel trained to do so.

The Health Care Management series is aimed at just such people: operational staff such as heads of departments or localities in purchasing or provider organizations, ward sisters/ charge nurses and their deputies who find that they are increasingly expected to deal with management issues which, until only recently, they were expected to refer upwards.

To complicate matters further such delayering of our organizations has come at a time of the most radical alterations to the systems for planning, commissioning and delivering healthcare since the service was founded. The National Health Service seems rapidly to be turning into the 'National Health Business' with an ethos and methods which feel alien to many of the staff expected to live with them. The boundaries between health and social services become ever more blurred as care is increasingly delivered in or near to clients' own homes, upsetting established patterns of working just as new and inexperienced managers take over the reins. The new organizations that have formed are undergoing a period of rapid learning and team building to undertake their new roles.

It is in such a context of rapid change that this series was conceived and it seemed thoroughly appropriate that the first title should be *Managing Change in the NHS*. The authors discuss the general skills and techniques that need to be employed in managing and sustaining change and illustrate their ideas with

ix

examples taken from their work in the service. They also explain those cultural and organizational aspects of the NHS which make it susceptible to certain conflicts and methods that may not be so relevant outside. The tribalism, the dominance of 'professionalism' and commitment to the process of actually serving patients (rather than profiting from them) are important drives that must be understood and harnessed to make progress. It is often this lack of sensitivity and understanding that makes some outside management consultants seem removed from the aims and values of healthcare organizations and which makes their advice more difficult to follow. Armed with the insights and techniques presented in this book healthcare managers should be better able to bring about the kinds of changes they know to be needed and to make them last.

Subsequent titles will reflect the general issues affecting all managerial or supervisory staff, as well as throwing light on the changes to healthcare in the UK to which they must respond. The authors have been chosen for their practical experience of dealing with these issues themselves, or of helping others to do so. The books in this series are therefore not academic treatises but working handbooks full of advice and practical aids. We hope that they will prove to be useful tools in the rapid personal development that will be needed.

Keith Holdaway
Assistant Director Human Resources
Mayday Healthcare, Surrey
1995

Introduction

In the last few years the NHS has had to change to an extent and at a pace that exceeds anything in its first 40 years of existence. There are very few parts of it that have remained untouched and many have been radically altered in at least some aspects. Against this backdrop of upheaval, the day-to-day work of treating and caring for people has gone on and has remained remarkably unaffected. The impact of managing this change has fallen heavily on the staff within the NHS and it is they who have had to juggle conflicting demands, rising expectations, policy changes and cost pressures while still making sure that the number one priority of patient care is delivered.

Our experience as training and development consultants working in the NHS has given us access to many change initiatives and projects and this book is an attempt to reflect on these, draw out the lessons learned and set these out in a systematic way as practical methods for managing change. Our experience has also taught us that there is no magic formula or simple prescription that will ensure success, and that alongside the systematic planning and practical methods there must be room for flexibility since the unexpected has a tendency to throw things into confusion. When this happens, those leading change must possess additional internal resources – qualities like innovation, humour, endurance and the ability to contain anxiety (others' and one's own). We have found that individual flexibility is increased by possessing:

- an understanding of the forces driving change
- a range of maps and models for thinking about change
- techniques for planning change
- skills in managing change projects

- behavioural skills in influencing change at the interpersonal level
- the capability to manage oneself.

In this book we will explore these ingredients using examples from our experience and organizing them into a framework that allows you, the reader, to have greater choice when engaged in the process of managing change.

In the first chapter we look at the context within which change is taking place within the NHS and chart some of the broad influences from a number of different perspectives. We then move on in Chapter 2 to explore the effects and experience of change at the individual, group and organizational level and pay particular attention to the fact that these reactions are critical determinants of the success or otherwise of change projects. Chapter 3 follows this theme by summarizing the success factors that people responsible for managing change have identified, followed by some of those factors which have the reverse effect.

Chapters 4 to 9 build up into a systematic approach to managing a change project. In Chapter 4 the key stages, tasks, roles and responsibilities are set out to ensure a solid starting framework from which you can work forward. In Chapter 5 we provide some methods of diagnosing organizational problems at different levels so that change can be correctly targeted and will address the root causes of these problems. Chapter 6 introduces the theme of setting clear goals and objectives for change projects and presents a practical technique that facilitates the development of goal setting. In Chapter 7 we present more practical tools and techniques for making the transition from the current situation with its identified problems to the desired goals which will remedy these. Following this detailed look at the changes which will need to be made, Chapter 8 looks at the way that change is resisted in organizations and provides typical examples of how this resistance may present itself, as well as practical methods that will help you to deal with it. Having planned and put into operation a change project, Chapter 9 covers the important subject of reviewing and evaluating change so as to ensure it achieves what it was intended to and also to ensure that learning is drawn from it for use in future change projects.

The final chapter moves on to looking at the role of the individual change agent (the person with prime responsibility for making the change happen) within change projects and explores some of the important personal management skills that will be required, making some suggestions as to how they can be developed.

Many of the chapters include practical activities for the reader to apply either to themselves or in their own settings, and case studies drawn from our experience as consultants which attempt to demonstrate key points we are making.

Acknowledgements

We would like to express our thanks to Dr Keith Holdaway, the series editor, for his advice and encouragement, to Sandra Dodgson, of the NHS Training Division, for her helpful suggestions and, finally, to our respective partners, Ian and Kathy, for their support.

Chapter 1

The Context of Change in the NHS

In this opening chapter we will look at the context of change from three different perspectives:

- very broad trends at a national and international level
- regional and localized changes that affect patterns of service delivery
- you, the manager, as the instrument of change.

The first two of these are important in understanding why change is happening and in positioning change projects to move in the right direction. The third is important in understanding your role and how this will affect any change being undertaken.

Without a clear understanding of these contextual issues it will be very difficult for you as a manager leading change to ensure that what you are doing fits with prevailing trends in the political and social environment, with local strategies designed to improve the health of your catchment population, with your whole organization's overall direction, with the aspirations and abilities of your staff, and finally with your own ability to deliver the change.

Broad Influences on Healthcare

As a manager leading change in your service you need to be able to understand, and explain to others, why change is happening and the likely directions that it will continue to move in. The current change issues such as organizational mergers, service retractions or developments, flattened management structures, changing skill profiles, inter-agency working, vocational and professional standards, etc. are not accidental and have their origins in a wide range of broader shifts and trends.

A useful model for categorizing such broad influences is the *PEST* analysis: this distinguishes *P*olitical, *E*conomic, *S*ocial and *T*echnological trends, although as we shall stress later all these categories interact as parts of a whole system. Thus a political policy change may be the result of prevailing economic conditions or recent technological discoveries rather than a totally isolated decision. We will now look at some of the recent and continuing issues that fall under each of these categories.

The political context

The NHS and Community Care Act of 1990 introduced the notion of an internal market by splitting the roles of purchaser and provider across what had previously been a level of management accountability. This together with the advent and expansion of GP fundholding, changes in the way that funding is allocated (to an amount per head of population), the shift towards primary care-led services and the continuing resettlement of long-stay patients into community-based settings, have significantly reshaped previous structures and relationships in the NHS.

Less direct changes which have had an impact on the NHS have been moves towards the market testing or contracting-out of public services deemed to be 'non-core'; in the NHS these have included catering, cleaning, laboratory services and increasingly include aspects of human resources, information, finance and even clinical services.

The general curtailment of trade union power and also to some extent the monopolistic power of the professions have all had effects on the service, resulting in things like Trust contracts and locally determined pay.

Similarly, the enshrining of social expectations of public services in The Citizen's Charter and The Patient's Charter has been designed to make services more accountable to their users and more transparent in their decision making and procedures. It is now a common occurrence for the decisions of individual clinicians and the policies and priorities of NHS organizations to be disputed and often legally challenged.

The parallel strengthening of audit requirements and mechanisms at clinical, managerial and resource levels has been part of an attempt to ensure public accountability while still allowing for more local decision making.

Changes in taxation policy such as the granting of tax relief to the elderly for private medical insurance have speeded up the move towards more private-sector provision, while changes in legislation on private-sector investment in the NHS have allowed joint ventures. The results of this are seen in the building of dedicated private patients units or wards within NHS hospitals and the supplementing of NHS resources through undertaking privately-funded work.

Britain's membership of the European Union is having an effect on medical training by bringing it into line with European requirements and on the redeployment of staff through regulations designed to protect previous employment rights (known as TUPE). Continuing trends will be likely to include the capping or setting of ceilings for management overheads as a proportion of total budgets, the movement towards a primary care-led NHS and perhaps a review of the current boundaries between Health and Local Authorities' Social Services departments.

The overall thrust in the political sphere has been to squeeze more out of the NHS by introducing a market-based system and to devolve accountability and responsibility away from the centre to a level as close to the patient as possible.

The economic context

Most of the world's developed nations are currently looking at ways to contain healthcare expenditure, whether they have private or publicly-funded systems. This has resulted in a variety of programmes, to ration or prioritize treatments, to set ceilings on procedure costs, deliver co-payment systems, achieve cost improvements and produce mixed economies of public and private provision. The increasing use of outcome research and health economics is a visible signal of the process of looking at both the clinical effectiveness of specific treatments and the relative cost-effectiveness of different treatments in an attempt to target spending where it will achieve the greatest health gain for the population as a whole. This has spawned a number of technical mechanisms for measuring healthcare interventions such as the *QALY* system (*Q*uality *A*djusted *L*ife *Y*ears) which attempt to integrate elements like cost, quality and outcome in order to aid decision making by policy makers and planners. These issues are increasingly taken into account when national and local strategies are set and will feed through into the contract-setting process over the next few years in terms of investment and disinvestment in specific healthcare interventions.

In the UK this takes place against a backdrop of trying to control public expenditure at a time of recession and to maintain a financial balance when there is a change in ratio between those in work contributing through the taxation system and those either unemployed, retired or young, who are drawing on the system. There is also the global situation of increasing competition in many sectors of manufacturing and technology from countries with much lower labour costs. This affects the long-term viability of the UK economy and the ability of the government to increase spending on healthcare in line with inflation and the combined effects of an increasingly elderly population and more sophisticated and expensive types of treatment.

Finally, as a response to economic uncompetitiveness and unemployment, the educational and training systems have been reformed to make them more vocationally-based and practically-oriented and to open up access to education for people who would not have fulfilled traditional academic requirements. This is having an impact in the NHS on professional qualifications where competency-based approaches are increasingly shaping the content and the process and highlighting areas of commonality between professions, and in areas previously neglected where people such as healthcare assistants are being offered the chance to gain recognition for their skills and abilities.

The social context

As just mentioned, the changing demographic profile in the UK means that the healthcare system is under increasing pressure. As the population lives longer, the costs of caring for vulnerable and chronically ill elderly people increases rapidly and out of line with other factors. These care needs fall on a comparatively smaller number of people in terms of both financial contributions and actual physical care giving. The effects of Community Care legislation and the general retraction from long-stay hospital provision means a very different pattern of care for these people and thus a need to change the type and method of service provision.

Various reports over the years have demonstrated the connection between poverty and ill health and, as divides in wealth continue to widen, the effect of deprivation on particular localities and on particular health problems will make itself increasingly felt. Changes in patterns of employment, with more part-time and predominantly female jobs and many males becoming long-term unemployed, will affect both the workforce profile and the incidence of mental health problems.

Another factor alluded to under political changes has been the general social trend towards both higher consumer expectations about services they receive and greater sophistication in terms of understanding and choosing what they need or want. The former has been enshrined in legislation like The Citizen's Charter and The Patient's Charter, with measures like maximum waiting times, complaints procedures, etc. The latter is seen in patients' willingness to challenge professionals' decisions or orthodoxies and to demand access to alternative or complementary approaches to healthcare.

Health and fitness as issues have a much higher profile with the general population than previously, as the proliferation of industries around sport, physical fitness, diet and emotional and psychological well-being demonstrate. This has raised people's expectations and feelings of control over health, increasing still further the effects just mentioned. Alongside this is a much greater awareness of the effects of the environment on health and a greater ability to identify and attribute mistakes in procedures either at the individual or the procedural level. This has increased the likelihood of litigation against individual doctors or healthcare providers and means that effective risk management is more critical to survival than previously; the sums of money involved can seriously undermine business viability.

Finally, the outbreak of new conditions such as HIV and AIDS has demonstrated that demands on healthcare systems are still subject to enormous fluctuations and mean that contingency plans and flexibility are necessary in even the most modern societies.

The technological context

Discoveries in the fields of medicine and healthcare are reshaping the NHS at an ever increasing rate and this looks likely to accelerate rather than decrease in the future. New methods of non-invasive surgery and developments in anaesthetics, for instance, can offer improved patient prognosis and mean shortened hospital stays and thus lower costs (although research is still continuing to quantify precisely these advantages and the knock-on effects in other parts of the system).

Similarly, new diagnostic, investigative and screening procedures using miniature cameras, scanning methods or genetic technology have opened up possibilities of earlier treatment or prevention that present both great opportunities to improve health and some threats in terms of spiralling costs, retraining of staff and moral and ethical dilemmas.

The ability to treat more conditions with drugs and medication rather than through operations or physical interventions will also mean shorter and less hospitalization although the cost of developing these drugs will be passed on by the pharmaceutical industry in prices, offsetting many of the cost savings.

The effects of many of these advances will be to extend the range of services that are carried out at a local level, whether this be in the patient's own home, the GP surgery or the local health clinic.

Information technology has been introduced widely and with varying degrees of success into the NHS. The demands for faster, greater and more accurate information are multiplied in a system that is more complex and fragmented (as a result of the internal market), where the sophistication of interventions is greater and where expectations are higher. This is a requirement which will continue to have a major impact for the foreseeable future. The ability to work at home and some distance from the geographical location of services through computers, modems, fax machines and other technology will affect the organization and administration of healthcare services. More sophisticated technology will even allow clinical interventions to be carried out across geographical divides and will mean dramatically different boundaries and frontiers in terms of provision and sharing of expertise.

Technological changes are perhaps the hardest to predict and of potentially the greatest impact and again require a high degree of flexibility and ability to respond quickly and effectively to change.

We have looked at some of the broader influences which are driving change in the NHS and outlined some of the impacts they are having. It is important that you bear in mind that all of these influences interact with each other to produce change in the whole NHS system. As managers leading change you need to be aware that change in one aspect or part of the total system will have some degree of impact on all the other parts, and that it is impossible totally to isolate change projects one from another or from the effects of broader influences.

The ability to understand and predict some of these impacts is important as it means you can steer change in an overall direction even if you cannot totally control it.

CHECKLIST

Answer the following questions in relation to change that you are managing or responsible for:

- Which factors in the PEST analysis are driving the change?
- Are there additional factors not mentioned?
- How are you taking account of these factors?
- Do you need to know more about some of these forces in order to manage change more effectively?

Local Influences

Some of the local influences driving change will be seen to be a translation of some of the broader influences, while others will be unique and particular, such as the arrival of a new manager or clinician, or the opening of a new facility or service. An analysis of the local influences obviously has to be done at that level and here we can only give suggestions and techniques rather than specific factors. The stakeholder analysis outlined in Chapter 5 is a useful starting point for exploring local influence.

Firstly, such an analysis requires good networks, through which information, often of the informal kind, can be gathered and exchanged. Such local networks provide excellent influence channels through which change can be facilitated and shaped in ways that are more subtle and less confrontational than more formal mechanisms. Effective managers of change in organizations almost invariably have access to these networks and have carefully built and nurtured them over periods of time. Such networks are the invisible glue that binds organizations together in ways that are more resilient and durable than formal structures or managerial lines of accountability. Sometimes these networks will be resisting change rather than promoting it, and a knowledge of how and why will serve to avoid stumbling into unnecessary effort and potential conflict.

Second, such an analysis requires making an accessible and usable chart of the influence factors involved. At the local level, we assume that there will be more of a balance between forces pushing for change and forces resisting change than there is at the broader level, where influences are generally moving in the direction of change. A useful technique for creating such a chart is the force-field analysis model developed by Kurt Lewin, who was an American practitioner, writer and researcher on group, organization and social behaviour. It is based on the assumption that any social situation is held in a state of balance by opposing forces, some trying to push the situation forward and some trying to hold it back. According to Lewin's model, change will only occur after the destabilizing of this balance by changing the forces on one side or the other. He found that it was far easier to remove resisting forces than it was to generate more driving forces – if you do the latter, the resisting forces increase in strength to compensate. The force-field analysis can be represented thus:

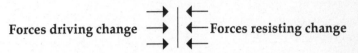

The situation

Forces driving change → | ← Forces resisting change

We recently worked with a clinical team whose local forces are represented on the following force-field analysis:

Driving forces	Resisting forces
• Pressure from other clinical departments to alter service	• Clinical outcomes satisfactory
• Need to exercise greater control over resources used	• Charter Standards being met
• Local GPs keen to offer aspects of service themselves	• Department unwilling to lose control and autonomy
• Purchasers not happy with service quality; threat of losing contract	• Sense of always having done it this way; why change now?
• Junior staff morale is low; many are disaffected and looking to leave	• Conflict between senior staff has led to impasse
• Need to provide more services in the community	• Fear of being de-skilled
• Newly appointed staff used to doing things differently	• Cost is a management problem, not the department's

As can be seen, these forces include both hard, quantitative factors and softer, qualitative ones such as relationships and individual perceptions. These softer factors are extremely influential and they should not be overlooked when managing change, which is after all as much about social systems and relationships as it is about technical developments or alterations.

At this point it would be a good idea to carry out a force-field analysis to determine what local forces are driving and opposing the change that you are involved in. To do this effectively you may need to gather together the project team (if you have one) or several people who complement your local knowledge so that you get as rich a picture as possible. It can also be helpful to stratify the analysis into individuals, colleagues, teams, departments, the organization and its immediate environment so that you have a more specific idea of where and what the differing driving and resisting forces are.

CHECKLIST

Ask yourself the following questions about your force-field analysis:

• How entrenched are the various opposing forces?
• Which ones are the most open to reduction?
• What influence networks have I got through which I can work on the resisting forces?
• Are there things I need to find out in order to get a clearer picture of the local level influences?

You as the Instrument of Change

Finally in this opening chapter we look at the vital role of the person leading change and how this is not a neutral position but a dynamic influence over the eventual success or failure of a project.

When leading change it is important to remember that you will be seen as a role model by others involved in it and they will look to you to determine how much you believe in it, your level of commitment and motivation, how well you handle the pressure and stress it generates and how you treat other people affected by it.

The way we behave in such situations is affected by the past, by previous experiences of change and transition and by beliefs we build up over many years about the way people, groups and organizations function, particularly when faced with extreme situations such as major change. It is worth remembering that we are undergoing change constantly in our personal lives and that most of our early and most powerful experiences of change take place in the family, school or college rather than in the workplace. It is these settings and experiences that largely determine our adaptive mechanisms of coping with the difficulties it causes and the sets of assumptions about what we can expect of ourselves and others in these situations.

These assumptions can be unhelpful when dealing with organizational change, since it is unlikely that colleagues and senior or junior staff will react in the way that family members or friends might do. Thus decisions based on these assumptions will be faulty and could well have unfortunate consequences.

As a person leading change, you need to consider how your individual personality will shape what happens. The clearer you can be in your own mind about your style and assumptions, the more you can consciously allow for them in your planning so that you are playing to your strengths rather than your weaknesses or blind spots.

CHECKLIST

Answer the following questions to help you clarify some of these issues for yourself:

- What do you feel have been the major change points in your life?
- How did you cope with/manage these changes? What themes repeat themselves?
- What subsequent beliefs and assumptions have you developed about yourself and others in light of these experiences of change?
- What do these tell you about the way you will go about managing change in the workplace?
- What pitfalls should you avoid? What strengths have you got to deploy?

Your answers will help you to build a profile of the influences which come from within you that will be operating in situations of change; this will allow you to predict and shape what happens rather than be driven unawares. In situations where you are managing uncertainty and anxiety, it is crucial that you are able to manage yourself effectively and to take active steps rather than be driven totally by events. We will look in the last chapter at some practical methods for building self-management skills.

Summary

In this opening chapter we have looked at factors which are likely to influence change, from very broad global trends, through local influences, to the very specific aspects of individual style and behaviour. In the next chapter we will look in more depth at some of the typical reactions you can expect from individuals (yourself included), groups and whole organizations when change occurs.

Chapter 2

Effects of Change on Individuals, Groups and Organizations

Change is, by its very nature, destabilizing. The 'givens' disappear and long-held beliefs may be called in to question. The world becomes less predictable, triggering the age-old human fear of the unknown. It is not surprising, therefore, that many people view change with considerable anxiety and try to avoid it if possible.

In order to operate effectively, we need to understand how the world around us works and to be able to predict fairly accurately the outcomes of different courses of action. For example, if you want some information you need to know who has the data and how they are likely to respond to your request for the details. When managing staff, you need to know which skills each member of your team has and to recognize that some may need to be pushed, while others need support. Tasks can be accomplished much more quickly and easily when you have this knowledge. A major organizational change could mean that you no longer know how to get the information you need, or that you are working with a completely different team and have to learn what each team member can do. Change can take us out of the known and the comfortable into a new situation where we must start learning again from scratch.

As we often prefer to stay with what we know, organizations

can become very static, failing to notice, or respond to, changes in the outside world. Gradually the organization can turn in on itself, becoming less effective in fulfilling its purpose as the environment changes around it. If no one notices what is happening, the organization may become out of touch with the people it is there to serve and 'die' as a result. As the world continues to change, different organizations will take its place. Alternatively, it may be forced to change by directives and demands from outside, causing dislocation and distress. Either way, some degree of change over time is inevitable, as the environment never stands still. Each change must start with destabilization, the necessary *'unfreezing'* of the situation which moves the organization away from the known and the predictable to enable change to begin. Although this is unsettling it can also lead to a sense of increased freedom, as some of the old rules are lifted, allowing room for development, creativity and innovation.

Responses to Change

Another consequence of change is loss, as any change involves the loss of the pre-existing situation. This can vary from loss of perceived status or preferred types of work, to loss of valued colleagues, to loss of a job or career. Whatever the loss, the initial situation in which the individual may have been quite comfortable is destroyed. The effect of this can be similar to bereavement. Elizabeth Kubler-Ross' work on loss has been shown to be applicable in organizational change situations (see Figure 2.1). Individual reactions may vary in intensity, and different people may go through the process at different speeds, but each person will typically go through the six stages described below.

Stage 1: shock

When an individual is first informed of a major change, they may be unable to take it in. They may say things like, 'I just don't believe it, it can't be true.' This stage is usually fairly short.

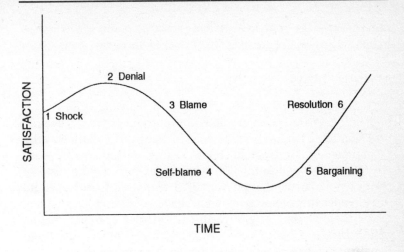

Figure 2.1 *Stages in the human response to change*

Stage 2: denial

At this stage the individual has begun to take in what has been said, but they are still unable to come to terms with the implications of the change. They may respond with a feeling that, 'Nothing will really be different' or, 'I've heard it all before; nothing ever changes around here, its all talk.' There may even be a feeling of euphoria, such as, 'I don't mind losing that task, I've got too much to do as it is' or, at the extreme, 'Redundancy will give me a chance to have a good break.'

This euphoria is generally short-lived and is an initial means of coping with the change, when admitting the degree of loss would be too much for the individual to handle. Occasionally, an individual can get stuck at this stage, unable to accept the reality of the change and make plans for the future. This may mean that they hold the department back, blocking others who are able to take the change on board and adapt to it. Alternatively, the effects may be largely self-destructive, as in the case of an ex-employee who continues to 'work' at his recent employers each day some months after redundancy, ostensibly using their job search facilities, but in reality trying to maintain his membership of the organization, denying that his employment there has ended. In either case an individual needs to be helped to move on through the process, towards acknowledging the reality of what is happening and taking control of his or her life again.

Stage 3: blame

At this stage the individual has begun to recognize what is happening and to feel angry about the change. There is a need to find a target for this anger, someone to blame: 'It's all their fault.' Sometimes individuals will choose to fix the blame on someone who is not the real author of the change; perhaps the head of their own department, with a cry of, 'If he was any use he would not have let this happen, he would have stuck up for us better.' Or all the members of a department can stick together, feeling 'got at' by the outside world: 'We might have known this would happen, the Chief Executive has always had it in for us.'

This can be the most uncomfortable and difficult stage to deal with as a manager or team leader. People may express their anger directly, as personal hostility, or they may be more passive, appearing to comply with the changes, but actually sabotaging them where they can. They may exert pressure on the team leader to collude with them in blaming the organization or run the risk of being considered a 'traitor'. This can lead to a conflict of loyalties for the manager, who may not be in total agreement with the changes, but knows they are inevitable. A balance needs to be struck between acknowledging people's anger, which can be a natural reaction to change, and preventing them from getting stuck in blaming others, which means that they will be unable to move on.

Stage 4: self-blame

At this stage people often move from blaming others to blaming themselves. They may feel that they have done something wrong to bring the change on themselves: 'If only I'd worked harder/ hadn't spoken out at the meeting, etc. then none of this would have happened.' Or they may feel unequal to the demands of their new situation: 'I'll never be able to work in this new way or learn these new skills, it's hopeless.'

This stage is usually characterized by feelings of despair or powerlessness and may, in some cases, lead to serious depression. At this stage people need support and encouragement and the team leader may need to find ways to enable them to rebuild their confidence and self-esteem.

Stage 5: bargaining

In the previous four stages individuals have been reacting to the impact of the change. At this stage they begin to adapt to the new situation, exploring the possibilities for different courses of action: 'What if I try this?' They may begin to develop new skills or build relationships with new team members if their old team has been destroyed. They accept that the old situation has gone and look at ways in which they can find satisfaction in the new circumstances.

This can be a very creative or developmental phase for the individual. These attempts to find something positive in the changed situation need to be supported by managers, so that individuals can move towards owning and being effective in their new roles and 'making it work' instead of going in for sabotage.

Stage 6: resolution

Finally, the individual has adapted to the changed situation and it has become the new status quo, predictable and perhaps even comfortable. Job performance should be at least as effective as it was before the change, perhaps more effective as a result of necessary changes in organization or skills. Ideally any change should be followed by a period of stability so that full adjustment can take place.

Factors Affecting Responses

As indicated above, all individuals will not go through this process at the same speed, or with the same intensity of feeling. Individual reactions will depend on a number of factors, which are discussed below.

Was the change imposed entirely from outside or did the staff members affected have some degree of choice or control over it?

When change is imposed, it often leads to a feeling of power-lessness, as people see themselves caught up in a larger process which takes no account of their views or needs. Radical changes may call people's key values and beliefs into question and may, directly or by implication, devalue the work they have done in the past: 'If it was really any good, why is it all being done away with now?' This will increase feelings of anger or despair.

On the other hand, if the members of a department have decided themselves to make a change there may still be some feelings of regret or ambivalence around, eg, anxiety about learning to perform a new procedure or a sense that the old rota system was personally more convenient than its replacement, but some sense of control will have been maintained and there will be some internal motivation to make the new system work. In the best circumstances, individuals may be able to make the change their own, using it as an opportunity to enhance their sense of purpose in work, to provide new challenges and to develop new skills.

How seriously is the person affected by the change?

An individual will obviously react more intensely if the change affects their life very significantly, eg, if their post is made redundant or the whole nature of their work changes as a result of a wider organizational change.

How have the individuals previously experienced change?

Have they found that change has sometimes led to new opportunities or have they felt that they have always lost out? Some people have a generally positive attitude to change and see it as exciting rather than threatening. Their self-esteem may generally be fairly high and they may have the confidence to believe that they will always be able to find a role. They may still have a strong emotional reaction but may move through it fairly quickly. Others may have experienced change after change and may simply not be able to cope with another adjustment, so they may become stuck in denial. Yet others may be predisposed to get stuck at the stage of blame or self-blame.

How much support is available to the individual in coping with the change?

If the rest of any individual's life is fulfilling and they have good support from family and friends in dealing with the change, they may again be able to adjust more quickly. If they have no support, or the work role was their main source of satisfaction and identity while other parts of their life were difficult, a change at work can be far more devastating.

The interplay of these factors will determine how a particular individual may react to the change. In an organization, however, the individual is not alone, and the reactions of colleagues, whose circumstances and predispositions may be very different, as well as the way in which the change is managed, will have a significant impact on the way an individual responds. We must now look in more detail at the impact of change on the functioning of teams, and of the organization as a whole.

CHECKLIST

The way in which any group or team will respond to change depends largely on its history and characteristics. You may want to think through where your own team stands on the following factors:

- Is the team long-established or relatively new?
- How cohesive is the team – are relationships between members close or distant?
- To what extent do team members support or compete with each other?
- Has the team faced change before – if so, how had it handled it?
- How much will the team's role or staff be affected, in practical terms, by this change?

Case Studies

To illustrate this, let us consider the contrasting ways in which three teams responded to change.

Team A

Team A had been established for nearly three years when it became clear that change was inevitable. The team's work could no longer be fully funded and there would have to be reductions in staff numbers, with the remaining team having to become income-generating.

Relationships between team members had never been close, as the team placed a value on individuals being able to operate independently, acting as a loose coalition rather than as a group. Individual team members also had different ideas about the way in which they should practise, which had been obscured by the fact that they operated semi-autonomously. The threat of change, and possible redundancies, brought out the competitive streak in team members, bringing differences to the surface. As the team tried to wrestle with setting a new sense of direction, individuals became increasingly hostile to one another, fighting to impose their ideas on the future of the team, thereby trying to ensure that they would be safe from redundancy.

The team leader did not have a clear idea on how the function could go forward, and contributed to the infighting by appearing not to treat team members even-handedly. He was fearful of the future and did not have the confidence to act as an effective advocate for the team in the wider organization. As the team created an atmosphere of collective panic, devoting more energy to its internal affairs than to demonstrating that it was needed and making positive plans for the future, it was eventually disbanded altogether.

Team B

Team B had been established for many years, with few changes in personnel; some of its members had been in the same team for most of their working lives. The team was hospital-based and very close-knit, with members sharing many of the same views and ideas on the way in which care should be delivered. Over the years the team had become rather insular and inward-looking, failing to take account of changes in accepted views of best clinical practice.

Eventually, outside pressure was put on the team to change its practice and restructure itself, to take account of the general trend for shorter lengths of stay for patients and more care delivered outside hospital settings. The whole team, including the leader, banded together to resist the changes, which threatened not only their established ways of operating, but also some jobs. They encouraged each other to believe that they could prevent the changes from taking place if they stuck together and defended their own view of reality. As the team refused to cooperate in any way with the changes, the Chief Executive decided to impose them. The team was amalgamated with another team which had taken a more realistic attitude in accepting that some changes were inevitable. The two leaders of the original teams had to compete for the management role in the new team, and Team B's leader lost out. The new team was restructured, with a number of Team B's original members losing their jobs, and the remaining members feeling that they had had little input in the shaping of the new working arrangements.

Through their failure to take account of changes going on around them and their refusal to consider any changes in their clinical practice or organizational arrangements, Team B had alienated the rest of the organization and thus reduced their own power to influence the shape of the changes.

Team C

A uni-disciplinary group working in community and clinic settings, Team C had also been established for a number of years, although there had been some changes in personnel as individuals moved on to further their careers and others joined the group. Thus some new ideas and approaches had been fed into the team over the years. Members of the team spent much of their time working independently, but they met regularly and provided one another with good professional support. The team leader ensured that these discussions also included reaching agreement on the overall aims and direction of the team so that members shared a sense of purpose.

Members of the team were, therefore, initially very angry when a change in priorities on the part of the District Health Authority purchaser meant that they would have to adjust their practice to give more emphasis to a different client group. They would also need to cut their costs or slim the department down. After their first reaction, they realized that some change was inevitable, and began to work together to find ways of making the adjustments which would still enable them to provide a service which would meet their own high standards. They succeeded in reducing costs by not filling some posts as they became vacant rather than through redundancies, and reshaped the service to meet the main changes, while gathering evidence to demonstrate the overall value of the service they provided. Their manager acted as an advocate for her department within the Trust, gaining the team time to shape their own re-organization, rather than having the precise detail imposed on them. Ultimately, although the team might say that the reshaped service is not their ideal, they would agree that it is a great deal better than an imposed solution and they are all committed to making it work.

These three case studies highlight a number of the issues which face any team undergoing change. The membership of the team may be thrown into question: who will belong to the new team? Individuals may find themselves cast adrift, either through redundancy or through reassignment to another team, losing their sense of belonging. There may be struggles for control of the team: who has the right to shape the future? The team may lose its sense of direction as the former certainties are disrupted.

Relationships between the team members will be spotlighted. If relationships have been good in the past it may help the team to deal constructively with the change; but there is a risk of 'group think', with team members colluding with each other in creating an unrealistic view of the future. If relationships have been distant or poor, then change will often destroy any sense of team spirit.

The team leader will often play a vital role in determining the impact these factors will have on the team, as the uncertainty of change will often make staff more dependent than usual on their manager. If the leader seems to be confused or lacking in direction, as in Team A, the team will often disintegrate. If the leader shares or promotes a negative attitude amongst team members, as in Team B, the team will fail to respond positively to the change. The leader can help the team to review its aims in the light of the change and to respond resourcefully to the demands of the new situation, as in Team C, allowing the team to come out of the change strengthened.

Effects on the Organization

When the change affects the whole organization, the effects of change on individuals and teams are multiplied many times. The resources which must be devoted to managing such a change, in terms of time, energy and sometimes money, are considerable and easy to underestimate. During the time of change, the organization will still have to provide a full service, within a finite amount of resources. It is, therefore, most important that there is a realistic timetable for the change project, and that the necessary resources are available.

Leadership of the whole organization is often even more vital than good leadership of individual teams. An organization can lose its way during a time of change, with different teams and departments pulling in opposite directions. The Chief Executive and board need to maintain a clear overview of the whole organization, pulling all the separate changes together. Rumours can abound at a time of organizational uncertainty, and good communication is necessary to hold the organization together. If the organization is able to manage change well, however, it can galvanize itself into action, enabling it to review its purpose and realign itself for a successful future.

Summary

In this chapter we have reviewed the effects of change on individuals, teams and organizations, and begun to see how the way in which change is managed can make a difference to the outcome. In the next chapter we will look in more detail at examples of successful and unsuccessful management of change.

Chapter 3

Successful and Unsuccessful Management of Change

The Change Equation

This is a list of key 'ingredients' for the change process, which is attributed to David Gleicher in Beckhard and Harris' book on change, *Organisational Transitions*. Written as an equation, the key factors look like this:

$$f(D,V,S) > R$$

This looks fearsomely mathematical, but it is actually a shorthand way of saying:

> In order for change to occur successfully, the combination of *D*issatisfaction with the present situation, a *V*ision of a more desirable future, and the knowledge of the first *S*teps to take in moving towards that future, must be greater than the *R*esistance to, or cost of, the change. If any of the first three factors are missing, then change will not take place successfully, no matter how strong the other factors are.

First of all, as the manager of the change, you need to look at your own position in relation to each of these factors.

CHECKLIST

- Are you dissatisfied with the present situation?

It may be that there have long been elements of the way your department works which have caused you concern, or it may be that external changes in the structure of the health service have caused you to realize that your department must change the way it works if it is to ensure its future survival. Either way, you need to believe that some elements of the current situation are unsatisfactory if you are to feel motivated in leading the change.

- Do you believe that the situation could be made better through a change project, and do you have a clear picture of this improved situation?
- Are you clear as to the first steps that must be taken to implement the change?
- What is your own level of resistance to the change?

Often, even when persuaded that change is a good idea, we still find it difficult, for all the reasons outlined in the last chapter. When starting a change project, it can be helpful to be honest with yourself about your own level of resistance.

- Are you convinced that the need to change and the prospects of a better future outweigh your resistance?
- If so, can you put your resistance to one side to enable you to lead the change project effectively?

When you have looked at all these issues for yourself, it is useful to assess how they will affect your team or department.

D = Dissatisfaction with the present situation

This is the factor most often overlooked by people managing change projects, but it can be the most crucial. If the people who will be most directly affected by the change are generally satisfied with the existing situation, they will have no incentive to change and may well be inclined to resist the change. As we saw in the previous chapter, change is always destabilizing and involves the loss of what may be a comfortable status quo. However attractive an alternative vision of the future may appear, people only tend to change when the current situation becomes uncomfortable. Thus, a first step in some change projects may be the generation of some dissatisfaction with the present state. There are a number of different ways in which this might be done. Sometimes simply involving team members in diagnosing the present situation will let them come to their own conclusion that all is not well. (A detailed discussion of organizational diagnosis can be found in Chapter 5.) There are situations where people are so unconvinced of the need to change that they are reluctant to become involved in the diagnosis, so other approaches have to be taken.

For example: perhaps you know that your team or organization needs to change its way of doing things because the outside world has changed and the purchasers or clients of the service are wanting different things. The group members may not see this because they are used to their way of doing things and have not seen how practice has moved on elsewhere. You would then need to challenge their insular world-view, perhaps by telling them about developments in practice elsewhere, or by getting them to go and see things working differently in another location. You might want to send individuals who are very set in their ways on secondment, or to bring people with experience elsewhere into your department, to increase the number of external influences.

If resistance still persists, you could get your group to do a 'doom scenario'. You would do this by first feeding in all the environmental trends and demands of key stakeholders and then asking the group: 'If these are the things that are going on around us, what will happen over the next few years if we just stay the same as we are now?' Faced with thinking this question through for themselves, the group members will often realize that to stay the same, while everyone around them is changing, could spell disaster for the department. Usually it will mean that the team will become progressively more out of step with its environment, until no one will purchase its services any more and it has to close down or be changed by force. Once people see this they will usually realize that the current situation will not be comfortable for very much longer, and so will become dissatisfied with it and wish to change it. Providing the structure for the group to think this future scenario through for themselves will be far more effective than simply telling them what the problems might be, as they will be more inclined to believe it if they have come to their own conclusions based on the evidence of future trends you provide. Be careful to ensure that your evidence is accurate, however, as you could soon lose credibility if you are seen to be scaremongering, and the group's complacency will increase.

Other, more drastic, ways of increasing dissatisfaction may include: starting disciplinary action for poor practice which might previously have been condoned; altering specific roles and responsibilities within individuals' jobs; or changing some working practices. All of these actions make the current, comfortable situation untenable. These methods should be used with caution, however, as they can make it unlikely that you will get cooperation later on in the change process, and if used without justification they can appear as victimization. They may be necessary on occasions where existing practice is very poor, or where resistance is very entrenched, with individual team members indicating that they are not prepared to engage with you in the change process at all. These methods demonstrate that you are serious about the change project. (Further examples of increasing dissatisfaction with the present situation can be found in a case study at the end of this chapter.)

V = A vision of a better future

Dissatisfaction alone is not sufficient to bring about change: people have to believe that the proposed change would lead to an improvement in their situation or service. Often individuals and groups hold on to highly unsatisfactory situations in the belief that, 'This is bad, but the alternative would be far worse.' It is thus important to have a picture of what the situation will be after the change, and to describe this picture in terms that make it as clear as possible for those undergoing the change, to make it almost tangible. It is even better to involve the people themselves in creating the vision of the future, if they are dissatisfied with the present and understand the need for change. This will give them a stake in that future picture and make them motivated to work towards bringing it about. (The use of the visioning technique with groups is described in Chapter 6.)

S = Knowledge of the first steps to take

Even a high level of dissatisfaction with the present and a rosy picture of the future do not guarantee a successful change project. It is necessary to have a plan for implementing the change or at least for the early stages of the project. Without this, the gap between the present and the future can seem so large that the group gets more and more disillusioned and dissatisfied, and they may start to take a range of ill-considered actions which are ineffective in bringing about the desired change. This is where the role of the manager can be particularly important in giving shape to the change project. (Chapter 7 covers the implementation phase of the change project in detail.)

R = Resistance to the change

Not only must all the other factors be present: taken together they must outweigh any resistance to the change. Earlier on, you examined whether you were convinced that this was so. It may sometimes be harder to convince other people, who may fear or dislike change. Increasing dissatisfaction with the present situation is, as we have seen, the first stage in overcoming resistance, but if it still persists you may need to employ some of the techniques described in Chapter 8.

People's Experiences of Change

The lessons that people learn from being directly involved in change projects are a valuable addition to the theories and concepts laid out in textbooks. Having looked at one overarching theory of change, we will now review the experiences of staff living through organization change, whether as managers of change projects or as team members undergoing change. In our work on organizational change within the NHS, we have often asked people what, in their experience, characterizes a successful change project. The most commonly mentioned factors in successful change projects are:

- direction
- timescales
- communication
- consultation
- resources
- making change real, and
- job security.

Direction

Under this heading there are a variety of subsidiary factors. One thing that is essential is a clear aim and objectives, which are understood by people throughout the organization. The frequently repeated statement, that if you don't know where you're going you won't know if or when you've arrived, holds true. People need to have a sense of purpose and direction in their lives and they need to have faith that managers leading organizations or teams through change are clear about where they're headed.

Underpinning this sense of direction is some understanding of – and hopefully agreement with – why the change is necessary. The more agreement you have the better; however, if you wait for full agreement you will never start a change project. To get to the why you need to have accurately diagnosed the current situation – this is outlined in Chapter 5. The level of detail that staff need about the aims is not so important. It can be unhelpful to involve people in too much of the minutiae as this dilutes the bigger aims with a clutter of smaller ones. Leadership is crucial in achieving a sense of direction and purpose.

Timescales

Time and time again we hear from managers that the biggest single reason for failure or less than successful change is unrealistic timescales.

Getting the right balance between challenging timescales that stretch staff and impossible ones that overstretch them is difficult but crucial. The commonest fault is setting tight timescales and then finding that deadlines slip; as a result, staff become disillusioned and demoralized and the change project and/or you as its manager lose credibility.

Another fault is not setting deadlines or allowing them to be pushed back, with the result that staff have no boundaries or parameters to work within. Having time boundaries provides a safety net or comfort zone that contains the anxiety of staff, which as we have seen from the previous chapter will be aroused by change.

When there are various threads to the change project it is helpful to produce a visual representation of the different timescales for each one. The simplest way is a GANT chart, which is outlined in Chapter 7.

Communication

It is all very well having clear aims and appropriate timescales but these have to be communicated, clearly and sometimes repeatedly.

Organizations undergoing change are perfect breeding grounds for rumour, innuendo and gossip, most of which come from people's uncertainty rather than the facts of the situation. It is important that misleading and anxiety-provoking misinformation is continually countered with clear and straightforward communication.

If staff suspect that there are hidden agendas or that they are being kept in the dark, this will be mirrored in increased levels of rumour and intrigue. People need information; if they are not given it they will create it for themselves.

There are a variety of channels of communication, from newsletters or bulletins to conversations in corridors. The communication channel you choose depends on a variety of factors; Chapter 7 provides a detailed communication plan.

Consultation

Staff will want to feel as though they are involved in the change project. This is natural and right since they have lots of expertise and experience to draw on. Not to do so is undermining for them and may have repercussions for their level of commitment to the success of the change project.

The crucial task is to consult and involve staff at the right points and levels in the project. The different levels of involvement and their appropriateness are dealt with in Chapter 8.

Consultation, however, is not always possible: in times of crisis you may have to act unilaterally and to consult would delay action which may be critical. To consult when a decision has already been made (because it is perceived to be the correct thing to do) is likely to result in both failure of the change project and in a more generalized loss of trust.

It is important to remember that there is a distinct difference between consultation and negotiation – in the former there is an implicit contract to canvas views without any obligation to act on them; in the latter there is an implicit agreement that some level of compromise will form part of any discussions. If staff perceive (rightly or wrongly) that their views will form a substantive part of any agreement then you, as a manager, risk conflict if your expectation is that you will merely canvass their views prior to making your own decision.

It is vital that you do not consult on issues over which you yourself have little or no control and that you don't make promises you are not sure you can keep.

Resources

Change always involves investment; of time, money, people, materials, buildings, energy, etc. When planning a project it is important not to underestimate the level of resources you need, where they will come from and how you will pay for them.

It is one thing for you to put in more work but you cannot expect the same sacrifices from people who don't fully own the change. Resentment quickly ensues if you ask for too many favours or trade on people's goodwill.

Similarly, if you ask people to do something but don't give them the tools to do it you will endanger your change project. Successful change management means accurately assessing the resources required, identifying the sources for them and securing their deployment.

Making change real

Nothing secures belief and commitment so successfully as seeing things change, therefore you need to make sure that some elements of the change happen quickly and visibly. For example, this might involve you yourself behaving in ways which are consistent with the change you are trying to bring about. Or it might involve new methods of gathering or coding information, adding additional elements to care programmes, drawing up standards about quality, skills, services, etc.

The important thing is that the changes are visible and symbolic or signify the wider-scale change project you are aiming at.

Job security

Many of the current changes in the NHS involve organizational mergers or reconfigurations of team and departmental structures. A particular feature of these are changes to the number and type of posts that are required, resulting in redundancy, early retirement, redeployment, recruitment and retraining. With such changes one of the critical factors that managers leading the change need to do is to define the new structure, identify staff required and to fill the new posts. Until staff feel some degree of job security they will not commit themselves to helping the change happen, or feel any ownership of it.

It is no use trying to generate a common vision if people do not know if they have any place in the new structure.

Other factors which are important but less often mentioned than those above are: ensuring that new working relationships are created that support the change, training people to perform new tasks and being tough-minded (not backing off when things get difficult).

Common Mistakes

To a large extent these are merely the opposites of success factors such as unclear aims, inappropriate timescales, inadequate resources, poor communication, etc.

There are however some common mistakes which have not been mentioned specifically which are worth emphasizing:

- knock-on effects
- contamination
- hijacking

- incorrect diagnosis, and
- a lack of ownership and commitment.

Knock-on effects

Managers often overlook or don't anticipate the knock-on effects of the change they initiate. We have mentioned that organizations are complex interactive systems and this means that change in one part usually has varying degrees of impact on the other parts, sometimes with very unfortunate consequences. Changes that at first sight appear small may, by the time they reach other parts of the organization, have assumed much larger proportions.

Contamination

Most organizations within the NHS are introducing a number of changes simultaneously, some larger than others, some quicker than others. A typical hospital change profile may resemble the model in Figure 3.1

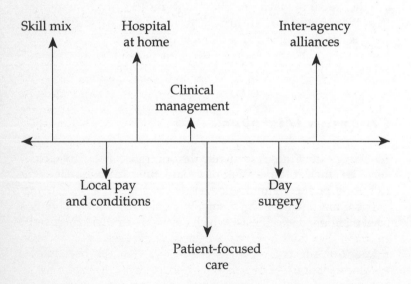

Figure 3.1 *Typical change issues in NHS providers*

It is easy to see that trying to isolate these change projects is impossible and that they must be managed in an integrated, coherent way. This requires strong strategic leadership, teamwork and communication, if some changes are not to get derailed by others.

Hijacking

Sometimes change projects are hijacked by those wishing to settle old scores or current conflicts not connected or relevant to the change. This is often because under the smokescreen of change such behaviour may not be noticed or may not be construed as vindictive.

Experience tends to show that although this may work in the short term, the long-term risks are heavy, including loss of trust or credibility, ongoing vendettas, sabotage further down the line, etc.

Once managers engage in degenerate behaviour then there is a risk of others copying it or it being seen as permitted or normal.

Incorrect diagnosis

Often the problem that the change project is attempting to rectify is wrongly diagnosed and the solution addresses the wrong thing.

When diagnosing work-based problems (see Chapter 5) it is essential to distinguish between the presenting problems or symptoms and the underlying problems or cause. An employee who arrives for work late or leaves early may be seen as having motivational problems when in fact they have some family crisis such as illness or divorce. It is tempting and often temperament-ally fitting for managers to make hasty diagnoses of problems so that they can 'do' something. It usually pays to be more careful and take more time over the diagnostic phase of change management.

Sometimes change has to happen not because of current problems but because managers must think ahead and position their services or organizations in anticipation of future problems (ie, changing consumer demands or expectations). So diagnosis has to be both present- and future-oriented, and must balance conflicting demands between rectifying past problems and meeting future changes.

39

Lack of ownership and commitment

Staff perceive the rapid turnover of managers in some teams or organizations as indicating a lack of ownership, commitment and continuity to the vision and aims. When this happens in conjunction with a change project, there is a strong feeling that it will be the staff who will be the ones around at the end ('to pick up the pieces') while the managers responsible will have moved on to other jobs or other organizations.

The factor of continuity needs to be borne in mind when setting up change projects and project teams. While one cannot guarantee staff continuity it must be seen as something to strive for during the change implementation.

The following case study illustrates the tension between the necessary requirements for change as indicated by the 'change equation' given at the beginning of this chapter and the desirable characteristics which those experiencing change would like to see. It particularly highlights the difficulty of achieving change when there is a high degree of comfort – and complacency – with the current situation.

Case Study

Care in the Community resettlement programme

As part of the national drive to close large Victorian institutions for people with mental health problems and learning difficulties, many Health Authorities have combined with Local Authority Social Services departments to create independent and autonomous housing consortia. These consortia are resettling patients from large institutions into small housing units within the community. We worked with the house manager of one such unit for people with learning difficulties to help him both with the change agenda for the house he was responsible for and with his own individual development as a manager.

He had a very challenging and exciting vision for the future of his service both in the medium and the longer term. Ultimately this would lead to a type of community outreach service for users where they would be leading largely independent lives with inputs from service providers only where necessary or where requested. In the shorter term it meant offering residents in the unit far more choice in their daily lives, much greater flexibility of routines and generally a reduction in the amount of intervention and bureaucracy.

The current situation

The problem or diagnosis of the current situation was that the institution had been recreated on a smaller scale in the community without any real or fundamental changes in the way that people behaved or the attitudes they held. The institution was within the staff and residents of the unit as much as in the systems and processes of the organization. The manager had developed some very practical steps which were designed to move the house towards the medium- and longer-term vision and tackle some of these problems. These included measures like re-organizing staff rotas so as to respond to the needs of the service rather than those of the staff; starting residents' and relatives' community meetings where views and ideas could be generated and discussed; organizing a staff development programme so that greater flexibility of work, tasks and responsibility was possible; and making certain structural alterations to maximize the privacy and autonomy of residents.

There was little overt disagreement from staff that the long-term vision was desirable and there were genuine attempts by the manager to involve all staff in the development of plans and policies that would build towards this. There was little problem with communicating the vision and plans since the staff team was small enough in number to have regular meetings and plenty of contact. There was wholehearted support from the wider organization – indeed it invested time and money in the service to make it possible (funding training, covering staff on training, etc). The likely implications of the changes were anticipated (such as the reactions of residents) and the timescales allowed plenty of leeway for sorting out difficulties and unforeseen problems. The resources which would be needed were evaluated and secured and milestones were set to chart progress. In short, a very thorough and thoughtful approach was taken that appeared likely to succeed.

Implementing the change

However, when the manager attempted to implement the changes he encountered a huge lack of enthusiasm and motivation from his staff to make things happen. Despite the apparent agreement, initiatives that were started quickly faded, or did not happen unless he was there to personally oversee them. Reasons were found why the new systems would not work and often these were claimed to be because the residents could not cope with them or that they were threatening the stability and security of the house. Much of the behaviour could be seen as passive resistance in that staff did not actively or directly refuse to do things or implement the changes. Rather there was a much more subtle process operating which had the same effects as outright refusal but was much harder to grapple with. Things had a way of returning to 'normal' as though nothing had ever happened to disturb the status quo.

When analysing this situation with the manager it was apparent that the staff were very comfortable with the current regime and that they currently felt little or no dissatisfaction with the way things were. The house was very much a 'closed system', with little or no feedback entering from the external environment. The drive to change was really perceived as the manager's own private agenda and not something that reflected any larger-scale changes about the way people with learning difficulties are construed or treated. It was obvious that in such a high comfort zone there was an enormous though largely passive resistance to change and moreover the collaborative, democratic and particip-ative management style being deployed was unlikely to work. The manager was disappointed because he had done all the things that staff usually want when encountering a change situation – consultation, clear communication, phased intro-duction, flexibility, etc – yet, as he saw it, staff were still not cooperating with the change.

This was a scenario that in terms of management of change required a much higher degree of dissatisfaction with the current situation to overcome the resistance to change. It is unlikely that such dissatisfaction would come from the residents themselves since they were not articulate and had been accustomed to being organized and directed by the system. In many cases they were also very comfortable with the situation since it met many of their basic needs and required only acquiescence in return. The dissatisfaction was not coming from the purchasers of the service since they were glad that the resettlement programme had happened thus far, had their hands full with the reconfiguration of their local acute hospitals, and did not have the detailed service knowledge to set exacting contract standards that would drive such change forward. Relatives of the residents were not dissatisfied since they could see all the basic needs being met and they were not presented with major intrusion or disruption to their own lives.

The way forward

Where, then, was the dissatisfaction going to enter the system?

The only way forward seemed to be a more vigorous approach to the situation by the organization and the manager such that the required changes become formalized in the roles and responsibilities of staff, and the introduction of some degree of performance monitoring to ensure the changes were happening. It was important that staff did not feel bullied by this new approach but it was similarly important that the organization signalled that it was moving forward and that it expected certain things of staff in their new settings that had not necessarily been expected before.

This proved impossible to achieve in the short term since, in examining the situation in more detail, it emerged that the housing consortia, although providing the services, owning the houses and employing the headquarters staff and care staff appointed since its founding, did not hold the contracts of most of the staff who had been transferred from health and social services along with the residents of the houses. The contracts of these staff awaited some detailed negotiation regarding transfer of pension rights previously accrued, etc. Since there was a no redundancy policy operating with one of the two employers, a fair number of staff had not yet decided which direction their careers should be going.

This also helped to explain some of the problems referred to earlier since not only was the dissatisfaction absent (rather the dissatisfaction was about being in some sort of career limbo) but staff could not fully identify or own the vision for the service since they did not belong to the same organization that had created it. Moreover, given their own uncertainty and the ambiguity of their contractual situation it was not difficult to see why staff motivation was poor. In such a circumstance the room for manoeuvre was very limited and it was unlikely that the resistance to change would be fully overcome until the contractual arrangements and obligations had been clarified.

However, the advantage in this situation was that in the longer term the house manager was able to build a much more flexible staff team since he was able to be much more specific and clear about expectations regarding the roles and responsibilities of staff and ensured that this was built into all new contracts as new staff were appointed or as existing staff transferred over.

In the short term, however, change was extremely difficult to achieve and had to be limited to what might be gained through softer interventions such as training and development, personal influence, generating enthusiasm for the future vision and harnessing positive elements within the staff team.

The key lessons from this case study are that:

- While change may be agreed to on the surface and seem like a good and desirable thing, it will not happen unless there is some real dissatisfaction felt within the organization or staff team.
- Where there are high degrees of comfort with the present situation, it will require an inordinate investment of energy to introduce significant change.
- If staff are outside the boundaries of the organization which is wishing to introduce change (or outside the team or departmental boundaries), change is again much more difficult to achieve.
- Resistance to change can be both an active or a passive process; if anything, the latter is more difficult to deal with since it is very hard to grasp what exactly is the precise nature of the resistance.

Summary

We have looked at the factors which managers and staff undergoing change identify as leading to success or failure in change projects. In the following chapters we will unpick the success factors and outline practical tips and guidelines that will help to ensure they are achieved.

Chapter 4

Managing a Change Project

In the last chapter we looked at some examples of well and poorly managed change. In this chapter we will outline the practicalities of managing a change project: the key stages, tasks, roles and responsibilities. This will enable you to develop an overall plan for your own change project. The following chapters will then cover each of the stages in more detail, guiding you through the management of a specific organizational change. We will start by looking at the key stages of any change project, which are shown in Figure 4.1.

_____ 1. Define the scope of the change project _____		
2. Diagnose the present situation	4. Analyse the gap ←— and —→ manage the transition	3. Create a vision of the desired future
_____ 5. Handle resistance _____		
_____ 6. Stabilize the new situation _____		

Figure 4.1 *The stages in managing a change project*

Key Stages of a Change Project

1. Define the scope of the change project

The purpose of the change must be identified, and the scope of the project defined. Key players, whose support will be needed or who may have the power to prevent the change project from succeeding, need to be involved at this stage. (We will discuss this stage later in this chapter.)

2. Diagnose the present situation

It is necessary to get a clear picture of the current stage of the part of the organization which will undergo the change, for it is more difficult to decide where you are going if you do not have a clear understanding of your starting point. This diagnosis may also make it easier to identify areas which, while not central to the change project, are nevertheless causing difficulties and could be revised as part of the overall change. This can help to gain commitment to the change project, using it as an opportunity to 'treat what hurts'. (The details of diagnosing the organization's present condition will be dealt with in Chapter 5.)

3. Create a vision of the desired future

A detailed picture of the desired future state needs to be built up. Often it is relatively easy to make the first few steps in a change, but the energy is then dissipated because no one has a clear idea of the final destination. Again, building a picture of an improved future can help to secure commitment. (Chapter 6 will deal with this aspect of the management of change.)

4. Analyse the gap and manage the transition

When you have a clear picture of both the current and desired future states, you know both the start and end points of the project. You could then compare planning a change project with planning a journey. Only when you know where you are and where you need to get to can you begin planning the route: 'If you don't know where you're going, any road will take you there.' Therefore, the fourth stage in managing a change project is to identify the gap between the current state and the desired future state and to plan the steps you will need to take to bridge it. At this stage you move from planning to managing the transition. (Chapter 7 will offer tools and techniques for this stage.)

5. Handle resistance

In looking at the effects of change on individuals in Chapter 2, we explored the reasons why people often resist change. Ideally, the sources of resistance to the change project need to be anticipated, and a plan evolved for handling resistance so that it does not hamper the progress of the change. (We will look at ways of handling resistance which emerges during a change project in Chapter 8.)

6. Stabilize the new situation

Finally, the change project needs to be evaluated and lessons learned for future change projects. The post-change situation needs to become established as the new status quo. (In Chapter 9, we will outline ways of keeping a change project on course and of stabilizing the new desired state.)

Defining the Scope of the Project

When managing organizational change, it is necessary to begin by defining the scope of the change project. This stage seems so obvious that it is often missed out! If attention is paid to defining the scope clearly at an early stage, it can minimize confusion and prevent unanticipated consequences of the change occurring at a later stage.

At the beginning of a change project, the individual or group responsible for managing the project needs to have fairly clear, if not particularly detailed, answers to the following questions. You will need to think them through for your own project.

What is the organizational problem which needs to be addressed by the change project?

Examples of problems which may necessitate organizational change are:

- the need to develop a new service to meet newly identified need or revised clinical techniques
- the need to restructure an existing service to meet the changing priorities of purchasers
- the need to cut costs
- the need to reorganize the way in which services are delivered to meet national or local targets, eg, Patients' Charter Standards.

Which parts of the organization need to change in order to address this problem?

- How extensive will the changes be?
- Will the change affect the whole organization or is it just one department or team that needs to change?

While it is important for the change project to have a clear focus, it is sometimes difficult to define the boundaries as changes in one department can have significant knock-on effects in other parts of the organization. This can cause serious disruption if it is not foreseen and planned for. A change project may be focused in one department but the effects of the change in linked departments need to be closely monitored.

What benefits will the organization gain by undertaking this change?

- Will it improve services or increase satisfaction for patients, purchasers or staff?
- Will it increase efficiency or reduce costs?
- Will it ensure financial survival for the organization?

These questions will help in assessing whether the change would be 'nice to do' or essential.

What will happen if the organization fails to address this problem?

This is really the negative counterpart to the previous question and the answer is sometimes called the 'doom scenario', as mentioned in the previous chapter. At this stage it is important to use this question to assess whether the 'problem' or need is sufficiently serious to justify the disruption a change project will cause. If the change is being imposed from outside the organization, there may be little enthusiasm for possible benefits of the change, but failure to change could have very serious consequences.

What are the likely costs of the change?

We have already seen that any change project imposes costs on an organization in terms of time, effect and disruption. The extent of these costs depends on how much of the organization will be involved, and how severely it will be affected.

- Will major restructuring or job losses be involved?
- Is serious resistance to the change likely?
- What level of resourcing will be required?
- How long is the change project likely to take?

Benefits of defining the scope

In answering these questions, you will be able to construct a project brief which outlines:

- the reason for undertaking the change; the problems which it will address and the desired outcomes
- the expected benefits and costs of the change
- the size of the likely change project, the resource implications, the broad timescales, and the extent of its effects on the organization.

As a result of doing this analysis, it may become clear that the costs of undertaking the change outweigh the benefits, and if the outside pressure to change is not strong, you may decide not to go ahead with the project. If it is clear that the change is necessary, you have now defined the scope of the project clearly. The document outlining the scope of the project will provide the basis for the more detailed project plan which will be drawn up when you come to manage the transition and implement the required changes. Before beginning the change project, however, you need to determine whether you need anyone else in the organization to support it, or to provide the resources to help you to manage it.

Roles and Responsibilities in a Change Project

Having completed the initial definition of the scope of the project, you need to allocate important roles and responsibilities. Getting the key people 'on board' right at the beginning can be vital.

Roles

Depending on the size of the project and its impact on the organization, the following roles may be useful:

- a project champion or sponsor
- a project steering group
- a project group
- specialist resources.

Project champion or sponsor
This would be a very senior manager or clinician who may not be directly involved in the project, but who will act as an advocate for it at organizational level. This role is useful if the change is supported within a particular department but lacks wider organizational support. It may also help the change to gain credibility within its own department if the sponsor is well-respected.

Project steering group
In a large organizational change project involving many departments, it is important to have a group of people who represent the various parts of the organization. This group sets

the overall direction for the change and helps to pull all the different threads of the change together. It can also monitor the progress of the project, ensuring that it is achieving its objectives. The group should include the project manager for the change as well as senior managers and those providing key resources to the change.

Project group
This is the group which has responsibility for the day-to-day planning and implementation of the change. It is led by the project manager and includes those directly involved in working on the change. In a smaller project, the project manager would manage the change alone, probably with occasional support from specialist resources.

Specialist resources
Depending on the nature of the change, the project manager may need access to specific expertise in, for example, personnel or finance. The people providing these resources may not be part of the change project full-time, but would just be brought in when required.

Responsibilities

In addition to these formal roles within a change project, different people will have different levels of influence and responsibility for taking decisions concerning the change. In order to ensure the success of the project, certain key people will need to be consulted or kept informed, while others take responsibility for implementing the changes. Time can often be wasted and change projects thrown off-course by a failure to involve key people at the appropriate stage. As you plan the different stages and tasks of the project, from the detailed diagnosis of the current situation, through the generation of the future picture, to the management of the transition, you may find it useful to draw up a 'responsibility chart'; a sample is shown in Figure 4.2 This indicates the level of responsibility the key people have for each task in the following five categories:

A – approve: powers of approval and veto
R – responsible for action and delivery of results once approval has been given

P – provide resources
I – to be kept informed, but otherwise not involved
C – to be consulted before decisions are taken.

There should never be more than one 'R' for each task. If you find that you are listing more than one person responsible for a particular task, then the task should either be divided in to two distinct parts and responsibility allocated for each part, or the 'R' should be raised up to a more senior management level so that one person has overall responsibility. Try also to keep 'A' to a minimum, otherwise it could be difficult to get a decision.

Figure 4.2 is a sample of a partially completed 'responsibility chart', indicating the broad division of responsibilities at the beginning of a project. As each stage of the project generates new tasks you may need to update the chart, or to divide the tasks up into smaller units. Timescales for the completion of specific stages can also be included.

People Tasks	Business manager	Ward sister	Senior staff nurse	Physiotherapist	Occupational therapist
Scope Change	R	A	P	C	I
Diagnose organization's state	R	C	P	P	P

Figure 4.2 *Partly completed sample 'responsibility chart'*

CHECKLIST

- Are you clear about the need for the change project?
- What benefits will it bring to the organization?
- What will be the likely costs of the change?
- Have you clarified the aims and scope of the project in such a way that these can be communicated to those who need to be involved?
- Have you identified the key players who need to support and steer the project?
- Are you clear who will manage the progress of the project on a day-to-day basis?
- Have you identified who will be responsible for the various key stages of the project?

Summary

Having defined the scope of the change project and identified various roles and responsibilities in taking decisions about the change, you have set up a skeleton structure for your change project. You are now ready to move on to the next stage: a detailed diagnosis of the current state of the organization. This will be covered in the next chapter.

Chapter 5

Diagnosing the Present Situation

A crucial element of successful change management is a clear understanding of why change is necessary. This understanding involves a diagnosis from a number of perspectives of the present stage of the organization or part of the organization. If done effectively, it allows problems to be targeted and knock-on effects to be anticipated and managed.

There are some important points worth remembering before embarking on this diagnostic phase:

- well begun is half done (a comprehensive diagnostic analysis is usually better than immediately jumping into the action phase)
- successful diagnosis uncovers the causes behind the problem as well as symptoms of it and distinguishes between the two
- the process of diagnosis works to clarify internal and external boundaries (within and between organizations and the environment)
- there is a need to be as clear as possible about the assumptions underlying the diagnosis (what makes organizations and people function)
- a diagnosis should be shared by as many of the involved parties as possible.

The Levels of Diagnosis

There are a number of levels of diagnosis and consequent change interventions. They all impact on one another and need to be looked at as interacting systems. They can be represented as concentric rings or orbits around the core of service delivery/patient care, as shown in Figure 5.1.

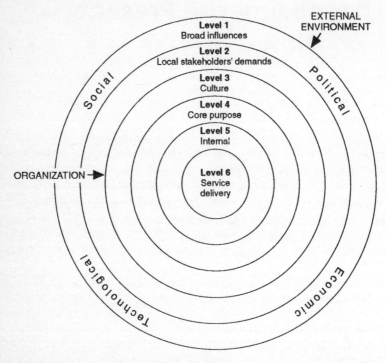

Figure 5.1 *The interacting levels of diagnosis*

Level 1: broad influences

The question here is, 'Is the organization being driven toward change by broad trends in its environment?' This will be uncovered by doing a PEST analysis as outlined in Chapter 1. The changes here may not appear relevant at first glance or may appear to impact only marginally on the delivery of care/service to patients. However, on more careful scrutiny it may be apparent that they are being filtered or translated by other rings in Figure 5.1. In a sense this level of diagnosis is less problematic than ones involving internal boundaries since it is very clearly 'out there'. However, while change may be non-negotiable at this level, there is considerable leeway for success or failure in how and when change is implemented within the organization or team.

Level 1 diagnosis will chart the very broadest changes and the long-term trends. It will not be sufficient as a diagnosis because it will not fit these trends into the local environment or the organization context itself. The change itself will be around environmental adaptation and doing this analysis requires an ability to scan the broad environment. A detailed knowledge of legislative changes may be essential.

Level 2: local stakeholders' demands

This level of diagnosis looks at actual entities which the organization is interacting with rather than broad trends and influences. The diagnostic process – known as stakeholder analysis or environmental mapping – attempts to chart important relationships between the organization and its key interfaces. The question here is, 'How healthy are the relationships between my organization and those outside who have a key influence/stake in my business?' An example of a stakeholder analysis for a Mental Health Trust might be such as that shown in Figure 5.2.

Having mapped the stakeholders, the next stage is to prioritize their relative importance to the organization on the criterion of, 'What will be the impact (strength and immediacy) if we fail to meet their needs/ignore them?' Finally, it is necessary to rehearse the demands from those stakeholders as accurately as possible and to look at how one's own organization is currently responding. The best way of doing this is to formulate them as though they were actually being put to you by the stakeholders concerned; for instance:

GP demand: 'We want to receive discharge summaries from you regarding our patients within 24 hours.'

Response: 'That's currently not possible to guarantee 100% of the time but we'll do our best.'

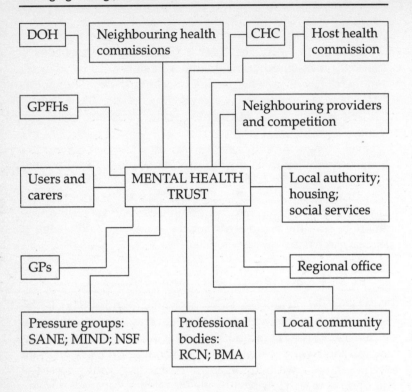

Figure 5.2 *Stakeholder analysis for a Mental Health Trust*

This exercise is very effective in bringing about readiness for change when done by groups or team within the organization because it forces them to take up external vantage points and positions. It requires people to step into others' shoes and see the requirements others have. It also makes explicit tensions and conflicts between different stakeholders' demands and the sort of compromises which must be arrived at to satisfy as many of the interests as possible. The change that will be required is repositioning the organization to meet the demands of its consumers and customers.

If you are part of a specific team or department, your analysis needs to take account of other parts of your own organization with which you interact in a customer-supplier relationship. For example, a ward's key stakeholders might include those shown in Figure 5.3.

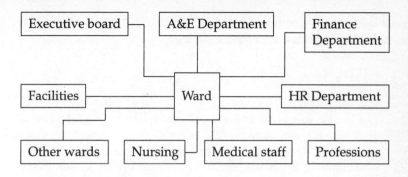

Figure 5.3 *A ward's key stakeholders*

Level 3: culture

With this level we enter the organization in its widest and most diffuse sense. An organization's culture is sometimes described as 'the way things are done around here'. It is the collection of norms, ground rules, dominant assumptions, tacit agendas, etc. that are built up over years of custom and practice. They can be likened to the submerged part of an iceberg, not visible but exerting powerful effects.

Culture is hard to see when you're part of it; often it is felt most clearly when you join an organization and are inducted into the dominant ways of behaving. Because of this, doing a diagnosis of an organization's culture often requires inviting someone 'objective' in, to comment on the way things are done or using 'objective' measurement instruments such as questionnaires or profiles. The question here is, 'Are the organizational norms and assumptions at odds with the way things now need to be done?' Currently many NHS organizations are attempting to remove layers of management and become less hierarchical and directive and more autonomous and facilitative (without sacrificing accountability) but they are doing so against a backdrop of a culture that militates against these new styles of management. It can be clearly seen that merely altering an organizational chart does not remove years of learnt behaviour or unwritten rules.

A change of culture within the whole organization or within sub-sections of it is a major but sometimes necessary goal;

however, it must be remembered that this order of change is long-term – years rather than months.

An organization's culture can be diagnosed in the following ways:

- Organizational members can review their cultural assumptions, norms and ground rules. To do this effectively they must temporarily 'step outside' the organization and reflect on it, usually with the help of an outside facilitator who will confront, challenge and hold a mirror up to the tacit ways of operating.
- Managers can use ready-made questionnaires or profiling instruments (often derived from organizational or occupational psychology) to plot their organizational culture. While no such test is going to be empirically valid in the strict scientific sense, they can be very useful as focuses or discussion points.
- External consultants can carry out a cultural audit through semi-structured interviews, observation of meetings and work groups and analysis of key documentation.

Having diagnosed the current culture, the change effect will be the renewal and replacement of key values, norms and ground rules with those deemed more fitting.

An example of a cultural constraint to change

A working example of a cultural barrier to change within the NHS can be seen in the attempted introduction of vocational qualifications (NVQs) into areas of professional practice such as nursing.

The dominant culture is one of lengthy and rigorous training and accreditation prior to being allowed to practise as a professionally recognized practitioner. One of the reasons that the introduction of NVQs has been resisted is that it challenges this dominant culture by raising a paradigm where staff must practise *before* they are eligible for accreditation. Professionals who are expected to train in this way to act as internal assessors often feel that this is back-to-front and might devalue the methods that they are trained in. This could contribute to resistance to NVQs both at the level of professional values and implementation methods.

Level 4: core purpose

At level 4 the key issue under scrutiny is, 'Has the organization correctly defined its essential purpose, the enterprise it is engaged in, and are its activities delivering this essential purpose?' This diagnosis will involve managers carefully exploring which parts of the organization contribute to this essential purpose and which parts do not.

It is commonly found that certain activities within organizations have grown from their origins in rather ad hoc or haphazard ways, or that their original rationale and justification have withered away. Similarly, it can be that activities have been developed because of individual/professional interests rather than to meet service needs appropriately.

The first piece of work at this level is to agree a common purpose for the organization (or a distinct part of it) by asking what it is actually there to do – not what people would like to do, or think they should do, but what they *have to do* to satisfy stakeholders' demands (identified in Level 2). This can be articulated in a brief and concise purpose or 'mission' statement. Once done, the separate activities of the organization can be scrutinized against this statement to see if they are contributing to it in an effective way.

The key change here will be the refocusing of activity on the essential purpose of the organization or unit within it.

Level 5: internal design

The penultimate phase of diagnostic activity is at the level of organizational design (again it can be applied to parts of the organization equally as well as to the whole thing). The key question here is 'Is the organization designed so as to deliver its objectives in the most effective and efficient manner?'

There are various models of examining organizational design. A robust yet simple one is that of Jay Galbraith, shown in Figure 5.4. To diagnose organizational design is to consider how well these five separate elements fit together.

Work and tasks

The work and tasks should be clarified from the analysis of the organization's/team's core purpose.

Figure 5.4 *Jay Galbraith's model for examining organizational design*

People
There should be the right number of people with the correct level of skills to carry out the work and tasks.

Structure
The structure should support these people with the right level of responsibility and accountability and should divide the work and tasks into whole jobs that have role clarity and coherence. Spans of control should be manageable and the structure should facilitate individual initiative and appropriate levels of autonomy.

Rewards
The reward system – both formal and informal – must reinforce and acknowledge the behaviours that deliver the work and tasks, both individually and across the whole organization. Reward systems must also ensure that the right people are recruited and retained and that people feel both valued and stretched to achieve more. They must also be seen as fair and equitable.

Information and decision making
Information that enables the work and tasks to be completed effectively must be collected in an appropriate form in a timely manner and it must reach the people who need to use it. Communication systems must keep people informed and foster

a feeling of involvement; they should not burden people with information that generates anxiety without action to deal with it. Decision making should take place as close to the level of service activity and implementation as possible, rather than at levels that merely reinforce status or role.

Degree of 'fit'

This level of organizational diagnosis can be done within the organization by reviewing the level of 'fit' between these elements and seeing where there is a clear mismatch. Examples of such mismatches might be where staff are on duty in times of low demand because they are paid overtime rates at these periods, or where information is collected for Korner returns which does not aid clinical care or decision making.

It should be remembered that once one element of the design fit is changed, it will automatically reshape the other four elements. Therefore any later changes in this fit must be carefully monitored to see how the other elements are reacting.

The change that will be planned following this fit analysis will be a redesign of the organization in terms of job design, skill requirements, roles and responsibilities, information needs and reward systems – a thorough overhaul of the systems and processes within the organization.

Level 6: service delivery

This final level of diagnosis will be most relevant to managers planning change projects within specific parts of the organization: wards, directorates, service areas, community teams, etc. Certain elements from the other levels are obviously relevant, such as the stakeholder analysis, the design fit and maybe even the cultural analysis. All of these can be carried out at a focused local level as well as at a broader organizational level.

There are however a number of other specific diagnostic questions and areas that need to be addressed at this service level; these are shown below.

Service delivery

Is the ward/department fulfilling its planned activity levels and performance against contracts? Is it doing this within budget limits?

Service quality
Is it delivering this activity in a way that meets the requirements of its consumers and customers? Considerations such as clinical effectiveness, value for money, speed of response and accessibility of the service will be important here.

Development capability
Is the ward or department thinking about its future capability requirements and making plans for ensuring these are targeted? Or is it merely focused on the immediate moment and the short term? Issues like succession planning and personal development need to be addressed here, as well as future positioning in terms of service changes, new technology, etc.

Communication
Is communication taking place effectively both in terms of content and process? Is the necessary data being captured and translated into information to be used in ways that facilitate decision-making, planning, monitoring and performance management? Is softer information working to make people feel included and involved within the team? Are messages from the outside world and the rest of the organization permeating through appropriately or are there significant distortions and time delays?

Team performance
Are the individuals and specialisms within the ward/ department, etc. working together effectively, or does their performance add up to less than the sum of the parts? Is there commitment to joint problem solving, an agreed sense of direction and a feeling of common ownership of issues, or does the team fragment under pressure?

Individual performance
What is the current level of morale and stress within the ward or department? Do people feel pressurized by work or under-utilized? Are people clear about their role, responsibilities and the performance expected of them? Are there particular inter-personal conflicts or suspicions and are these affecting the rest of the team?

Cohesiveness

Finally, is there an overall sense of cohesiveness and trust within the ward/department? Do people forgive mistakes (provided they are not repeated) and are people willing to make appropriate levels of sacrifice for each other in time of need? Is it a rewarding and satisfying place to work and do people speak about it positively?

Case Study

Change in primary care

As part of the overall transformation which is currently taking place within healthcare, many changes are happening in primary care, particularly general practice. We will use these changes as an example to illustrate the use of the different levels of diagnosis in defining how an organization needs to change and putting that change programme into operation.

Level 1: broad influences

These are often divided into four main areas:

* political
* economic
* social, and
* technological.

Some of the key trends which most affect primary care in each of these areas are discussed below.

Political The expansion of the fundholding scheme and of plans to involve all GPs in locality-based purchasing, means that each practice will have to take on increased responsibility for taking decisions on the shape of secondary-care services.

The plans to move services from hospital settings to community and primary-care settings mean that GPs will become involved in multi-professional teams providing a range of services, and that they will also often have to provide more intensive services for patients discharged earlier from acute care, or from long-stay institutions.

The targeting policies of other agencies may leave GPs to provide services to those who were unable to get assistance elsewhere.

Economic The way in which GPs are reimbursed for their services was altered in the revised contract, introduced by the government in 1990, with, among other things, more emphasis being placed on health promotion. Plans to equalize reimbursement for staff between practices has created some 'losing' practices.

With their involvement in purchasing, GPs are increasingly involved in making decisions about the allocation of resources, and choices about which services should be provided, where and for whom.

Social GPs report that patients are becoming more demanding, wanting a wider range of services, and are more aware of their rights since the introduction of The Patients' Charter. With the increase in demand for alternative and complementary medicine, some practices are contracting with practitioners such as chiropractors and homoeopaths to provide a service from practice premises.

The ageing population, coupled with the policies on community care, means that GPs will be involved in giving increased long-term care for patients with chronic conditions or severe disabilities.

Technological Advances in medical technology mean a wider range of services to choose from, both in terms of secondary-care referrals and the services that can be provided within primary care. Some practices now have ultrasound machines or provide minor surgery. Developments in information technology have seen almost all practices become computerized to some degree in recent years, and with the possibility of direct links to the FHSAs, some practices are planning to become paperless. Possible future scenarios include consultations by computer link.

These are only a few of the environmental trends which are currently affecting primary care. Cumulatively, they mean that it is no longer sufficient for GPs to focus on direct patient contact, as they have an increasing role in shaping the services provided by other groups or agencies. They are now part of a multi-disciplinary team providing an increasingly diverse range of services, and they often find themselves heading an organization composed of a wide range of different professions and staff groups. Members of the other professions and staff groups have to find their own places within the organization. Thus these trends provide the driving forces for organizational change. As mentioned in Chapter 1, these and other trends are affecting all parts of the health service, and it is important to examine the precise effect they will have on your organization when planning any kind of change.

Level 2: local stakeholders' demands

The broad influences mentioned in the last section will be common to all practices, but the precise effects of these trends will depend on local factors. For example, one practice may be in an area with a high and growing proportion of residents over the age of 65, while another practice may have a young population in its catchment area, with a growing birthrate and a high level of social deprivation. Both practices may introduce additional services, but those services will be different. Equally, the targeting policies of Social Services departments in different areas may differ, as may the relationships practices have with other agencies. The configuration of other health services will vary between areas, with implications for the services the practice decides to provide on its own premises. Again, these are only a few of the potential local stakeholders, and each organization would need to do its own environmental mapping, as outlined in Chapter 5.

Level 3: culture

In the past, the culture of GP surgeries has often been very individualistic and practices have functioned more as alliances of separate practitioners than as organizations. With the development of the idea of the primary healthcare team, where practitioners from different professions provide an integrated service, and the increasing responsibility for the future planning and shaping of services, this culture of individuality is no longer so appropriate. Many practices are starting to develop a team approach, both amongst the partners and amongst the whole primary healthcare team and the practice staff group. With the increasing diversity of responsibilities, from fundholding to computerization to the development of services within the practice, it is no longer possible for all the partners to have equal knowledge of all areas of the practice's operations, and so responsibilities have had to be divided up. This has further broken down the individualistic culture, with one partner often having to act on behalf of all of the others, and even to examine the others' clinical practice in terms of resource allocation. This change is still taking place in most practices, and has not always been easy or painless.

Level 4: core purpose

Practices still have the key purpose of providing primary healthcare services to their local residents, but many of them have widened their definition of this purpose, so that they aim to become 'one-stop shops' for healthcare. This will obviously have direct implications for the range of services provided and the links between different services.

Level 5: internal design

As the range of services provided increases, and there is a need to carry out an ever-increasing range of managerial and administrative tasks linked to fundholding and to the need to record and provide more information, practices are having to change their internal design.

The larger practices are developing management structures which comprise not only practice managers and fund managers, but also nurse managers and, sometimes, managers for the other services provided from their premises, such as counselling and mental health services. There is a need to develop and clarify the roles and responsibilities of these new managers, and to sort out the boundaries between their authority and that of the partners. In addition to employing their own staff, such as practice nurses to provide additional services, practices are also increasingly providing a base for staff employed by other NHS organizations, for example community nurses, and for self-employed practitioners such as counsellors, who provide a service to practice patients. There can be difficulties in forming a team when its members have different external loyalties and, often, different terms and conditions. Practices are having to develop as organizations sophisticated enough to manage these different relationships. There is also the development of information technology, requiring staff with new skills and changing the way certain tasks are carried out.

Thus all practices will have to examine not only the new work and tasks, but also the people and skills required to carry out those tasks, the organizational structure which will help the practice to manage its workload, the information which needs to be available to enable people to make the correct decisions, and the rewards which need to be offered to attract the right people. The current changes will not leave any of these areas untouched.

Level 6: service delivery

These are the detailed changes that a practice may decide to make to the way it provides its service. They may range from a change in the way reception is organized and run, to a decision to provide a new clinic for asthmatics, for example. The precise changes should depend on the practice's analysis of the needs and demands of its stakeholders and fit with its own view of its core purpose. These changes will be the ones that patients see, and should be supported by changes at all the other levels, such as improvements in teamworking. If the practice has worked through all the levels of diagnosis, these changes should improve the services provided and make the practice more effective at meeting patients' needs.

Changes will continue to occur in primary care, so the practice will need to keep a watchful eye on broad environmental trends and on the evolving demands of its stakeholders, in order to keep adjusting its services to meet the requirements of the environment.

This analysis shows how organizations in primary care might use the different levels of diagnosis. Any organization or department, large or small, needs to look at these different levels when facing change, and can follow a similar process. Take some time to think through the implications for your organization at each of these levels.

Summary

We have looked at a number of different levels of diagnosis and various techniques and processes for carrying them out. These are not mutually exclusive but rather cumulative, and you may need to apply several levels of diagnostic analysis to your particular organization or piece of it. Some of the diagnosis you can carry out yourself; some is better done by a team or group who are involved in the change; some can be done using instruments like questionnaires; and some is best carried out using external people.

At the end of your diagnosis you should be able to formulate the problem that the organization is faced with in a succinct and precise way that people can understand and hopefully agree with. If it is accurate then it should make people less satisfied with the current position because they can see the need for change. At the end of the diagnostic phase people are ready to look forward to what the new situation might look like.

This vision of the future and the dissatisfaction with the present are two of the three essential ingredients in what Kurt Lewin called the 'change equation' (see Chapter 3). The third ingredient for achieving change is a knowledge of the practical steps to take to achieve the vision. When combined, these three ingredients must outweigh the resistance to or cost of change.

We have looked at ways of highlighting dissatisfaction with the present; we will look in the next chapter at what the solution might be in its broadest terms. Following this we will look at practical steps for realizing this future picture.

Chapter 6

Change Goals

Many change projects fail because no one is clear about the ultimate goal of the change. Without such a goal, the organization can 'tack' somewhat aimlessly from one small change to another, perhaps attempting to 'fix' problems as they appear, with no overall sense of direction. One short-term 'solution' can give rise to new problems which require more adjustment. There will be more energy in, and commitment to, the change project if it is seen to be leading towards an ultimate goal of importance to the team or organization. Visioning can be a useful technique for generating such goals. It invites team members to cast their minds forward to create a picture of an ideal future. The more practicable elements of this picture can then be drawn out and used as the basis for building up a plan for the future.

Visioning

Although visioning has recently acquired a reputation in the NHS for being something of a consultants' gimmick, there are a number of reasons why you may want to use it as a basis for defining your change goals. It has the advantage of being able to help people to break out of familiar ways of thinking, and allows future plans to emerge which are more radical and not simply extrapolated from the past. Incremental changes, small adjustments of the current situation, will not be sufficient to allow the organization to cope with the radical changes taking place in the broader NHS environment.

The technique can be particularly useful if you are dealing with a demoralized team who are finding it difficult to come up with creative solutions to the problems presented by change, or dealing with an imposed change where there was little dissatisfaction with the original situation, so the attitude to the change is one of resignation, rather than a will to drive the change forward. If team members are involved in developing the vision, the process can generate great enthusiasm and commitment to turning the vision into reality, as well as giving people back their sense of choice and ability to influence their situation.

There are, however, certain situations where it would be inappropriate to use the visioning technique. It can only be used when there is genuinely some leeway for a creative approach to the situation, as it will soon be recognized as a sterile exercise if there is no likelihood of influencing the change. It is also unsuitable to ask people to try to create a vision when they are uncertain of whether they will be candidates for redundancy. Creative thinking requires a measure of security, and staff will be unlikely to have much enthusiasm for generating a vision for an organization of which they may not be a part. It would be counter-productive to use visioning with individuals or a team who are stuck in the denial stage of the human responses to change (see Chapter 2) or who are reluctant to recognize the realities of the current situation. Thus although it can be a very useful technique, some judgement needs to be exercised in deciding when to use it. Some of the poor reputation of the technique may be attributable to its use on the wrong occasions.

Using the Visioning Technique

This technique can be used with a group or on your own. The following instructions are for use with a group, but can easily be adapted for individual use. The technique has eight distinct stages, discussed below.

1. Invite group members to imagine, for example, their ideal organization, if the change is organization wide, or their ideal

service for a particular group of patients, if that is the purpose of the change project. Explain to them that they can be as visionary as they like at this stage; evaluation comes later. They should not concentrate on resource restrictions or on what is achievable within a particular timescale. Instead they should try to imagine in detail what their ideal service would be like. What would it offer service users? What sorts of people would be providing the service? How would it be structured and organized? What would it feel like to work in the service? The aim here is to get the vision as clear as possible in individuals' minds.

2. When people have had a little time to create their own visions, each individual should be invited to take a large piece of paper and some marker pens and to draw a representation of their vision of the service. People often have difficulty with this, fearing that their drawing will not be good enough. They should be encouraged to draw if at all possible, as once people try to describe their visions in words, they often start editing them and evaluating them, whereas drawing often leads to more imaginative representations. It should be made clear that the reason for drawing is to enable team members to picture each other's visions, and that artistic ability does not matter.

3. When individuals have finished drawing their visions, ask them to talk them through with other group members. If the group is larger than eight to ten members, you may need to divide it initially into sub-groups for sharing. Discourage people from criticizing each other's visions at this stage.

4. When everyone has talked their drawing through, work with the group to identify any key similarities or differences between the visions. Are there any common elements? Are there any ideas which, although contributed by one person, are of immediate appeal to the majority of group members? Are there any major areas of disagreement? Is it possible to arrive at a composite vision, building on the key ideas from all the individual visions? It is important to discuss the issues emerging from this exercise fully, particularly if there are major disagreements about the vision. If there are no major disagreements, a great deal of excitement and enthusiasm can be generated in swapping and building on each other's ideas. Everyone's contribution to this

process should be acknowledged, in order to build the sense of ownership. End this phase of the process by drawing all the common threads together into a composite picture of the group's ideal future.

5. When a shared long-term vision has emerged from the discussions, it is necessary to bring a more realistic focus to the process. Taking the composite vision, which of the key ideas can be used as a basis for long-term (say, five years) aims for the group? It may be that the kernels of even the more radical ideas can be used to provide aims. There can be a tendency for the group to become depressed at this stage as they realize that their vision will not be directly achieved in its original form, but if they allow their thinking to remain relaxed and creative they may be surprised at how many of their ideas can be included, even if in an adjusted form. In order to keep the team focused, the ideas should be boiled down to around three aims, which would take the team a significant way towards the achievement of the vision.

6. When the aims have been agreed, the next stage is to derive some shorter-term objectives from the aims. This may be done by the group as a whole, or particular individuals may be asked to take the aims away and to work up objectives from them. As a rough guide, two to three objectives should be derived from each aim. This would give a maximum of about nine objectives. Often NHS organizations generate long lists of objectives, reducing the chances of achieving the main targets, so it is often preferable to keep the list shorter and determine key priorities when choosing between different areas which demand attention. The objectives should take the group or organization towards achieving the long-term aims, and be achievable within, say, a year. Further objectives can be set in following years to take the organization closer to achieving the aims.

7. Although the objectives should be derived from the aims to make sure that they take the organization in its determined direction, at this stage it is important to refer back to the diagnosis of the current state of the organization. The objectives need to be set to enable the organization to make good progress towards its aims within the year, but also to take into account

where the organization is starting from. They should be challenging but not unrealistically ambitious.

Clear objectives may be set using the *SMART* formula. This suggests that objectives should be:

Specific   – what precisely will be achieved?
Measurable – how will you measure success?
Achievable – are the objectives realistic?
Relevant   – do the objectives deal with things which are important to the organization?
Timed   – are the objectives achievable within a specific timescale?

8. Finally, the objectives should be agreed by group members, and cleared with other parts of the organization if necessary. An action plan can then be devised for implementing them and the group can take the first steps towards the achievement of its vision of the future service.

Thus the vision can be used as a basis for deriving aims, objectives and an action plan. The process of using the visioning technique is illustrated in Figure 6.1.

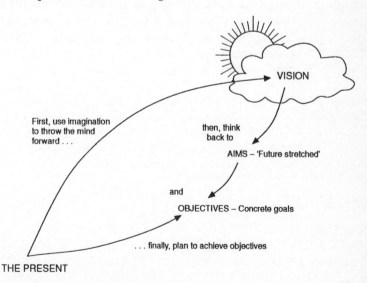

VISION

First, use imagination to throw the mind forward . . .

then, think back to

AIMS – 'Future stretched'

and

OBJECTIVES – Concrete goals

. . . finally, plan to achieve objectives

THE PRESENT

Figure 6.1 *The visioning process*

Case Studies

Changing childbirth

A maternity unit within a Women and Child Health Directorate needed to update their service in response to 'Changing Childbirth' (a paper on the future of maternity services, which recommends that the services become more responsive to individual women's wishes) and to changes going on within the local service.

As the unit had had a reputation for being a little old-fashioned in their attitude to services, they could have viewed this as a threat, but they were able to use the visioning technique to clarify their own values and beliefs about the ideal maternity service. The vision aimed to keep the service hospital-based, but to increase the personal contact between the mothers and their named midwives and to enhance choice for mothers concerning the management of their labour.

The team found that using the visioning technique enabled the more reactionary team members, who had been doubtful about changing the service, to feel some sense of control over the changes and to design them in a way that retained some of the values which were important to them. The team were able to use the vision to define their aims for the future of the service. They could then set some short-term objectives which enabled them to manage the change without external intervention.

Transfer of services from acute to community

A combined Acute and Community Trust received a strategy document from the local DHA which indicated that the purchasers wished to transfer resources from the acute to the community sector over a period of some years.

The Trust worked to create a vision of the future relationship between the acute and community services within their organization, incorporating wide-ranging changes to the way in which services should be delivered. They decided that they would gradually build on their presence in local health centres and clinics to provide a service located in a chain of polyclinics with an 'in-reach' service at the main hospital site. They shared elements of the vision with their purchasers, who, while not accepting all the elements immediately, were impressed enough to use some of the ideas to form part of their acute services review.

The use of the visioning technique thus enabled the organization to influence their future in a way they would not have done had they waited for the purchasers to complete their review. They also were prepared for some of the results of the review and could set objectives to enable them to implement some of the necessary changes.

This visioning technique can be adapted for different situations. If the change project is short term it may be helpful to invite participants to envision the ideal service created as a result of the change and then to derive shorter-term change objectives directly from the vision, without needing to go through the stage of developing five-year aims. If some change is inevitable, but there is some leeway for the department concerned to influence some of the details of the change, then visioning can still be used within the given parameters to enable some creative input from the department concerned. This was used successfully by Team C in the case study given in Chapter 2.

It can be used to provide a framework for problem solving. For example, if the maternity unit discussed received an unexpected bequest, they might refer back to the vision in deciding how to spend it and use it to make a contribution towards enhancing their community service. The visioning technique can also be used to help individuals define career goals, inviting them to envision their ideal job, again drawing out the aspects of the vision which may be achievable, and then deriving a career and personal development plan. Thus it is a flexible technique, which can help people to re-establish a sense of direction in difficult or confusing situations

Situations where Visioning is Inappropriate

As we indicated above, there are some situations where visioning is inappropriate. This is often the case when the goals or even the details of the change are prescribed, particularly if they form part of a nationally determined plan, and there is no scope for introducing any creative ideas. Using visioning there could give staff unrealistic expectations and prevent them coming to terms with the realities of the situation. In these situations it is best to be honest about the fact that the change has already been determined, and to ensure that everyone is clear about the goals to which they must work. You can then move straight on to analysing the gap between the current situation and the prescribed goals, and to planning the detailed implementation of the necessary changes. When it is impossible to use visioning to gain ownership of the changes you may need to spend more time overcoming resistance to the change. We will look at these two areas in the next two chapters.

Summary

In this chapter we have looked at a technique for arriving at a broad vision of how an organization, service or team would like to develop. We have then outlined how change goals can be derived from such a vision, which are realistic given the organization's current situation, but will also take it part of the way towards the agreed ideal future. In the next chapter we will move on to look at the practical implementation of these change goals.

Chapter 7

Managing the Transition

Following on from the last two chapters, you should now have a clear picture of where the department or organization is now, and where you would like it to be after the change. It is the transition between these two states which you are now faced with managing. In this chapter we will look at managing the transition in detail.

From the visioning and future planning exercise you should have some clear long-term aims and some short-term objectives. These may provide you with a clear indication of what the organization needs to be able to do, but not of how it needs to change in order to achieve this. In order to become clearer about the specific steps you need to undertake in changing the organization, you will need to undertake a 'gap analysis'. This involves taking different aspects of your original organizational diagnosis and looking at how each would need to change for the organization to be able to achieve your objectives. It fleshes out your vision, aims and objectives, giving you a more detailed indication of the kind of organization you will need to create. This will give you the steps of your change project – the smaller transitions that you will need to manage in order to achieve your overall goals. Let's now go through the different levels of the diagnosis you made for your change project, outlined in Chapter 5.

Level 1: Broad Influences

Although you might wish to alter them, there is probably little you can do about these broader, longer-term trends. You just need to ensure that your change project is in line with them. Hopefully, you will have taken them into account when bringing your vision back down to realistic aims (see Chapter 6).

Level 2: Stakeholder Analysis

This level is important, as any change in your organization or team will undoubtedly cause changes in your relationships with your stakeholders. It is often easy to get so caught up in the internal management of the change project that its effect on external groups and organizations is forgotten; many organizations have found that they run into trouble and opposition because they have failed to consider these effects or have failed to communicate their plans properly. Some of these effects will be intentional and may, in fact, be the whole point of the change project, but others may be less desirable. With your key change aims and objectives in mind, refer back to your stakeholder analysis, look at your relationship with each stakeholder in turn and ask yourself these questions:

- If the organization changes to meet our objectives, what effects, both positive and negative, will this have on our ability to meet the demands of this stakeholder and on their perception of us?
- How would we ideally like to respond to the demands of this stakeholder and can we use this change project to move towards this ideal situation?

The answers to these questions will suggest actions that need to be taken in order to use the change as a positive opportunity to improve your stakeholder relationships or to minimize the negative effects of the change for your stakeholders. For example, if you believe that the change will improve your services, but realize that it will initially cause some disruption, you may need to give some thought to how you will explain the ultimate aim of the change and outline the benefits that you believe it will bring, as well as looking for ways to minimize the disruption. We will look in more detail at communication planning later in this chapter.

Level 3: Organizational Culture

Organizational culture is difficult to change, because it comprises the underlying beliefs and assumptions of a group of people about the right way to behave, the right way to see the world, 'the way things are done around here.' These cannot be changed simply by management instruction or by rearranging the structure. Unfortunately, culture can often be a major factor in sabotaging change projects, because if, as a result of the change, people are being asked to act in ways that contradict their basic beliefs about 'the way things should be done', they are unlikely to be successful in changing their behaviour effectively. Although the NHS is a strongly 'values-based' organization, often it is not people's conscious values, which they may argue strongly for, which cause the major problems, but more the underlying norms, which they may not be aware of nor able to articulate clearly, but which will still govern their behaviour.

One of the main ways of trying to ensure that the change project and organizational culture can work in the same direction rather than opposing one another is to involve as many of the people who will be implementing the change as possible in the planning phase. Aspects of culture will often surface during the visioning exercise, when people start to say, 'We can't do that, it will never work'. Often asking the simple question, 'Why?' will help to make an implicit belief explicit. It is sometimes useful to follow an idea back along the chain, by continuing to ask, 'Why?' until you cannot go any further. The final statement which can no longer be reduced to a more fundamental statement is probably an indication of an underlying belief shared by many people in the organization. This can be a difficult process, as people will find it uncomfortable to question things which they have held to be self-evidently true, but it can also be liberating, allowing people to consider options they had previously thought to be impossible.

Do not forget that you too are a member of your organization's culture and share its beliefs to at least some degree, so you may have to stop yourself from reacting instinctively to discount ideas and force yourself to question your own beliefs! This is why it can sometimes be useful to have help from an outside consultant when dealing with issues of organizational culture: they may be able to distinguish assumptions from facts more easily than someone from within the organization. As it is impossible to work with culture until the underlying assumptions have been surfaced, it is worthwhile maintaining a slightly questioning attitude to your own assumptions throughout the project. It may provide you with some useful information as to what may be going on in the organization.

As mentioned at the beginning of Chapter 2, people need a degree of predictability in order to function effectively. The norms that make up an organization's culture provide that stability and predictability. If the culture is not conflicting with the change or causing serious problems, then it is generally best to leave it alone.

Level 4: Core Purpose

During your diagnosis you will have reviewed your organization's or department's core purpose. You may have concluded that your original core purpose is still appropriate in the current situation, and that the focus of the change should be on the way in which the organization works towards achieving that purpose. In that case the only action you need to take at this level is to ensure that everyone has a clear understanding of the organization's or department's purpose, and knows how their changed role will contribute to the achievement of that purpose.

Alternatively, you may have decided that changes in the overall environment mean that the organization is now meeting different needs and, therefore, has a different core purpose. The recent health service changes provide an example of this: the role of District Health Authorities was changed from the management of services to the purchasing of services for a particular population; many Health Authorities reviewed their core purposes and worked to clarify their understanding of their new role. They found that the change in purpose meant that different tasks had to be undertaken and new skills developed. If you find that your department's role and purpose has changed, then you need to work to clarify this with your staff, so that they understand what the team is now trying to achieve. A change in your organization's core purpose is likely to mean that there will be significant changes in the tasks to be performed and in the design of the organization to achieve that purpose. Thus you will need to ensure that you design the organization or department to fit in with its new purpose and that you again make it clear to your staff how their new roles will contribute to achieving the organization's purpose.

Level 5: Internal Design

This level is the start of the detailed implementation of the change. It can be tempting to jump straight in at this level, with the practicalities of the change. It is important, however, to pay attention to the preceding levels as they set the context for the change and give it a direction. Sometimes clarifying the broader context of the change can help to reduce resistance, as people can understand the reason for the change and will be less likely to see it as a whim of management. It can also be a mistake to concentrate exclusively on the other levels, as people will soon become suspicious of too much discussion of culture and core purpose, if they see no practical action. For change to work, all the levels should be linked together. Thus the design of the organization needs to follow from the core purpose.

Whether your group or organization has changed its core purpose or not, you need to start by determining what work the organization needs to undertake in order to achieve its purpose:

- What are the key tasks which must be performed if the organization is to be effective?
- What are the key differences between these new tasks and those currently being performed by your staff?
- How does the way in which the work is organized need to change so that these tasks can be performed effectively?

- What action do we need to take to move from the way we are currently working to the way in which we need to work in the future?

If you are managing a major change project, the key tasks may be significantly altered, whereas with a smaller project the main focus of change may be the way in which existing tasks are organized and performed. Either way, you need to be clear about the initial steps you need to take to start to bring about the change in the work and tasks undertaken by the organization or department. It may be easier to become clearer about this when you look at the implications of the changes in work and tasks for the other elements of organizational design:

- people
- structure
- information and decision-making processes
- rewards.

People

- Do you have the right number of people in the department to carry out the new tasks?
- Do those people have the required skills or is there a need for some form of training or development, or for changes in skill mix?
- Does the allocation of responsibility for particular pieces of work need reviewing to ensure that individuals and teams have responsibility for whole tasks and to increase efficiency or effectiveness?

Again, use the answers to these questions to help you to enumerate the actions that you need to take in managing the change project to ensure that the people you have in your team or department are able to carry out the new tasks.

Structure

This is generally adjusted as part of any change project, and altering it can make it very clear that change is underway. Changes in structure by themselves are, however, unlikely to achieve major changes in the organization's performance or role. If the people with the right skills to do the new job are not present, reshuffling the existing staff into a new structure is unlikely to make much difference. Structures can also make completing the main tasks more difficult: for example, multi-disciplinary teamworking is becoming more and more important within the NHS and rigid structures based on individual departments or professions can be a barrier. Any structure will facilitate some channels of communication and block others, so when altering your department's structure it is important to ask the following questions:

* Does this structure help or hinder the completion of the key tasks?
* Are key people in the right places in the structure?

Information and decision-making processes

If new tasks are to be carried out or work is to be organized in a different way, then it is likely that there will be new information requirements and that decisions may have to be taken in different ways. The answers to the following questions should help to clarify this:

* What information is required to complete the new tasks and how can you ensure that you obtain it?
* What decisions need to be taken on a regular basis, and at what level in the structure is it most appropriate to take those decisions?
* How can you ensure that those people taking the decisions have access to the necessary information?

Rewards

Do not forget to consider informal rewards, including praise and the opportunity to do interesting work or projects, as well as formal rewards contained in pay and conditions.

* Does the current rewards structure support good performance in the new work and tasks or does it contain perverse incentives?

- How does the rewards structure need to be changed so that it reflects the new situation?

Level 6: Service Delivery

At this most detailed level you can look at specific changes that need to be made to:

- the mechanics of service delivery within the ward, team or department, to meet revised activity targets and stay within budget limits
- the quality of the service delivered, to meet new stakeholder requirements
- the flexibility or development capability of the department – will this change leave it able to adapt further to meet future demands?
- the communication systems within the department and between departments
- the way in which the team works together, and its morale and cohesiveness
- the performance of individuals within the team or department.

Action Planning

Having worked systematically through the changes that need to be made at each level of diagnosis, you should now have a list of steps you need to take in order to implement the change successfully. You now need to turn this list into an action plan. Look at your list and try to place the actions in order:

- Do some of the actions follow a logical sequence, with the completion of one being necessary before you can begin the next? In general, the broader steps, such as reviewing the core purpose, should come before and inform some of the more specific actions such as reallocating particular tasks.
- Do some of the actions need to run concurrently (eg, related changes in different departments or teams)?

- Are there any actions which are crucial to the success of the whole project?
- What are the likely timescales for the completion of individual actions?
- What is the overall timescale for the completion of the whole project?

You can now put an action plan together, assigning an order and timescales for completion of the individual tasks. Be as realistic as you can about how long particular tasks will take, as it can damage the credibility of the entire project if timescales are continually slipping. You may find it helpful to represent your action plan in graph form, as in the example shown in Figure 7.1

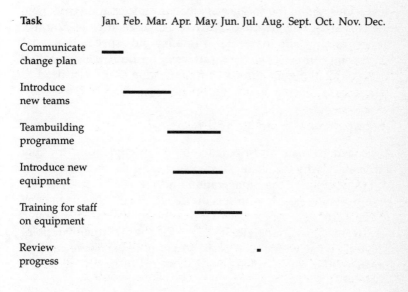

Figure 7.1 *Sample action plan*

This kind of chart helps you to see at a glance the progress you should have made at any given time in the change project. Depending on the overall timescale, you may need to divide it up into weeks rather than months. You can use this in conjunction with the responsibility chart that we looked at in Chapter 4

(Figure 4.2) ensuring that each task is clearly assigned to a named individual. If you are managing a large change project, try not to take on more than you can handle. You may want to take charge of any actions that are crucial to the success of the whole project and to delegate some of the others. It is important, however, that you maintain an overview of the whole project and make sure that all the tasks are being carried out to plan.

The Communication Plan

One of the key parts of any change project is communication. Sometimes this is considered so important that a separate communication plan is drawn up. Change makes people very suspicious and in the absence of any clear information from you, the grapevine will go into overdrive, damaging morale. You will never totally eliminate the rumour and speculation that accompany times of change, but you can limit their negative effects by having an agreed communication plan. You need to take decisions on the following key points.

What do we need to tell people?

You need to maintain a balance between explaining the 'big picture', ie, why the change is necessary and the overall benefits of the change for the organization and the people it services – and providing people with specific details of how the change will affect them: ie, their jobs, the kinds of work they will be doing, new teams or locations, etc. Try to see the change from their point of view: what would you want to know if you were in their position? Can you involve people in any of the planning for the change?

When are we going to tell them?

In the early stages of the change project, before all the details are fully worked out, people may well come to believe that there is a 'master plan' which you are being secretive about. Thus, the earlier you can communicate clear information the less time there will be for rumours about this 'plan' to run rife. While you are at the stage of having no clear decisions to communicate, it can be helpful to outline what you are doing in diagnosis and to make it clear when you will be in a position to make a decision.

Who is going to tell them?

Depending on the scale and importance of the change project, you may hold a large meeting where senior managers outline the overall plan to all staff, or you may decide that it is better for managers to brief their own departments in the more informal setting of a team briefing, where people may feel more comfortable in asking questions. The most important thing is that all of the people who are involved in communicating the change give a common message.

How are we going to communicate?

You may decide to use a newsletter to keep people informed of the general aspects of the change, but call meetings to announce specific decisions. Where decisions have a serious impact on individuals, changing their roles or even leading to redundancies, you will also need to have individual meetings. All these elements can be incorporated into your communication plan.

Summary

In this chapter we have worked through all the different actions you will need to take in order to achieve your change goals, and drawn up a detailed action plan for the change project. We have also looked at developing a communication plan to keep others informed about the change. Now you have planned how you will manage the transition between the organization's current state and the desired new situation, you can proceed to implement your plan.

It is important to keep your plans under review, as they will inevitably need some adjustment during the implementation phase. In the next chapter we will look at one of the factors most likely to alter your plans – resistance to the change – and how you can work with and overcome it.

Chapter 8

Overcoming Resistance to Change

Resistance to change is, to some extent, natural and inevitable. As we noted in Chapter 2, change is destabilizing, and both organizations and individuals will often react initially by striving to retain their equilibrium. If you refer back to the force-field analysis in Chapter 1, you will see that it is often better to work on reducing the resisting forces from the outset, rather than building up the driving forces and trying to push the change through: this will often have the effect of building up the resisting forces, and equilibrium may be maintained with worsened organizational relationships.

Some Useful Techniques

The following techniques can be effective in gaining commitment to change and thus reducing resistance:

- involvement
- visioning
- communication
- 'treating what hurts'
- addressing the readiness and capability of individuals to change
- encouraging people to develop new relationships.

Involvement

Try to involve the people most affected by the change in diagnosing the present situation and identifying the problems or issues which need to be tackled by the project. This will help to convince people of the need to change and give them some sense of control over the areas which the project will cover. (Chapter 5 covers this in more detail.)

Visioning

Where appropriate, use the visioning technique to allow people to shape the future and to gain a sense of ownership and commitment to the future plans. (Chapter 6 describes the technique.)

Communication

During the implementation of the change, ensure that you maintain good, clear communication at all stages to prevent rumours creating a climate of fear, as people will often resist anything they have little information about. Much resistance to change is built up as a result of poor communication. (We discussed the communication plan in Chapter 7.)

'Treating what hurts'

Try to make change less painful by 'treating what hurts' as part of the change project, ie, where possible use the general change as an opportunity to sort out a problem that has been bothering people for some time, to let them see some positive early results from the change. Early successes can often make a great deal of difference to staff's perceptions of the overall change, particularly if they can gain some of the credit for these successes themselves. The uncertainty caused by change can threaten individuals' self-esteem, so if they can feel boosted by something associated with the change they will have more commitment to it.

Addressing the readiness and capability of individuals to change

It is often helpful to try to analyse why individuals are resisting change. Sometimes people are fearful of change because they do not feel that they will be able to cope with the new demands being made of them, so training and other forms of support can reduce resistance as individuals become confident in the new skills. Other individuals may be very influential in their peer groups and it may be important for you to get them on your side if you can, so that they can become advocates for the change. You may find it useful to use the chart shown in Figure 8.1 to identify where you need to put your effort.

Individuals	Readiness			Capability			Clout		
	High	Medium	Low	High	Medium	Low	High	Medium	Low
Team leader			×	×			×		
Sandra Green	×					×			×
David Brown			×			×		×	

Figure 8.1 *Sample readiness and capability chart*

In this situation, the team leader, who should be driving the change, is both capable and influential but is not enthusiastic about the change. You would need to spend some time trying to influence her into changing her opinion of the change. Why is she so resistant; does she perhaps perceive the change as detrimental to her status or to her department? Is there anything you can do to turn her from a loser into a winner?

Sandra Green, a member of the team, is enthused by the change but lacks the skills to be able to implement it. You do not need to spend time trying to influence her, but you may need to provide her with training or development to prevent her enthusiasm from turning to concern when she realizes what will be required of her. She is a new member of the team and so is not particularly influential. She will not be able to act as an advocate for the change with the others.

David Brown is unenthusiastic about the change and also lacks the skills to carry it out. However, he is a long-serving member of the team and has the respect of the other team members, so it could be important to try to change his attitude so that he will at least refrain from rubbishing the change. Is he resisting the change on principle or because he fears he will not be able to carry out the new tasks? It may be worth providing him with some training as well as trying to influence him.

You can use a similar chart for your key individuals to look at where you should be devoting your time and whether the problem is one of readiness or capability to change.

Encouraging people to develop new relationships

Encouraging people to develop relationships with new colleagues – the new teams which will support the change – can be of great importance as the new social system in the organization can become self-reinforcing (Chapter 7 discusses the last four points in more detail.)

All these aspects of managing a change project are designed to ensure that, although people may initially perceive the change as a threat and a wholly negative experience, they move first towards an understanding of why the change must take place, then to some sense of control in shaping the change, and finally to a sense of ownership and commitment to the change as they begin to see some positive results from the project. They may even find that the development of new skills and the development of the organization leaves them with an enhanced feeling of self-esteem after the project. This is the ideal situation but, as we have seen from the case studies, progress through a change project will not always be so smooth. Resistance to the change may become more entrenched for various reasons. We will now look in more detail at some of the reasons for resistance, and how such resistance can be managed.

Causes of Resistance to Change Projects

The main causes of resistance to change projects are:

- lack of understanding
- fundamental disagreement with the philosophy of the change
- disagreement with different aspects of the change, and
- personal loss.

Lack of understanding

If the change is a fundamental one, or the group or department concerned have become set in their ways, they may be unable to visualize or believe that the service can be that different. Change can sometimes involve a 'paradigm shift', a move to a different way of seeing the organization or service. In this case it may not be sufficient simply to reiterate that things will be different: people may need to go through a learning process in order to be able to understand and believe in the change.

Different people have different ways of learning about change. Some people need to read about the effects of a similar change in operation elsewhere through a case study, or even to see the change up and running in another organization, and to think through for themselves how such a change might impact their department or organization before becoming directly involved with the implementation. Other people need to understand the theory behind the change and to be convinced that it is well thought through and based on a sound conceptual under-standing of the values and structure of the service. Yet others will need to experience the change for themselves before they can believe in it, either through role play or simulation exercises, or even by secondment to another organization where the change is already in place. Finally, more practical people may be most convinced by being involved in a pilot project, implementing the change in one small part of the organization or service to examine how it will work and suggest improvements, or in planning the detailed implementation of the change. Thus you may need to use different methods to enable different people to understand the change and their role in its implementation, to free up their thinking and enable them to believe that change is possible. These different ways of learning about change are based on Kolb's theory of learning styles, which can be applied to all forms of learning. Please see the Further Reading section at the back of this book if you would like to know more about this work and its uses.

Fundamental disagreement with the philosophy of the change

Individuals may have a fundamental philosophical disagreement with the aims of the change project. The NHS is a values-driven organization and people often feel strongly about the philosophy underlying their work. Thus individuals may resist changes such as the recent reforms to the health service and the introduction of Community Care because they feel them to be misguided and wrong.

If you are faced with implementing a change in such circumstances, there may be little you can do to reduce the resistance. You may hope that you can persuade the individuals concerned that they are wrong about the change, or to demonstrate to them that it does not have the negative effects that they suppose by showing it working in another location or trying to bring them on board once the change is up and running. Although it is sometimes possible for people to be won round or to change their beliefs, if the difference is really fundamental it is unlikely that you will convince them in a short period of time. They may well obstruct efforts to implement the change, creating a serious problem for you. If you are certain that the change is important or essential, you will need to limit the damage these people can do to its successful implementation. It may be possible to work round them, so that they are marginalized and have little chance of disrupting the project. If they are in key positions it will be necessary to demonstrate to them that change is inevitable and that they will have to choose whether to work within the changed situation or to leave the organization.

Disagreement with different aspects of the change

As the NHS is such a values-driven organization, individuals may sometimes couch their resistance to change in terms of philosophy and values, when in fact they really dislike some aspect of the change plan or the way in which it is being implemented, or fear that they will lose out as a result of the change process. It is, therefore, worth investigating the real issue which is causing the resistance. People can be resistant to different aspects of the change project. They may, for example, not disagree with the underlying philosophy of Community Care, but they might disagree with the plans to create large group homes in the community, or with details of the closure plan for a psychiatric hospital. Or perhaps you have persuaded staff on the wards of the need to collect good clinical information, but have asked for the information in a format which they find time-consuming and difficult to produce, so they are not entering the data. Thus people may be resistant to the underlying philosophy of the change, or the strategy of the change plan, or to specific tactical details.

It is worth spending some time to identify the cause of the resistance rather than assuming that you know what it is. You can then decide whether you can alter the change project in any way in order to reduce the resistance. You are unlikely to change the basic philosophy or goals of the project, but you may be able to alter some aspects of the strategy or, even more likely, some of the details of implementation. Where it is possible to do this without serious damage to the project, it is generally worth doing so, as meeting people's needs or allaying their fears can be a very good way of reducing resistance, rather than turning the dispute into a trial of strength which you will only win at great cost to the organization. Wherever possible in the change process, try to turn losers into winners.

Personal loss

There will be some changes where it is inevitable that there will be losers. This is true where the change involves people having to change their jobs, perhaps having to accept lower-graded roles, where people have to compete for fewer jobs, and where there will be redundancies. In these situations it is best to be honest with yourself and other people about the nature of the change, and not to use the techniques aimed at gaining commitment to the change with people whose jobs may be at risk, as you will only increase suspicion and anger. When people are uncertain whether their future lies within an organization, they will not be interested in defining the vision for a change of which they may not be a part. Their main need is for reliable information. If their future depends on a new structure, then that should be published as soon as possible; if on the location of a new headquarters, then that should be decided with all speed. Long periods of uncertainty sap morale and build up a feeling of mistrust which can continue even after the change is over and even amongst those who are not selected for redundancy. It is better to be clear about the changes, even though that means imparting bad news.

It is also preferable to get the unpleasant and difficult phase of the change, the stage of loss, over as quickly as possible, while being as fair as possible to those people who will leave. It is important that the process is seen to be fair and that proper selection for redundancy takes place. The correct balance between allowing people to get over the shock of losing their jobs, and prolonging the period during which redundancies take place is difficult to achieve, but still worth attempting, both for the individuals concerned and for the health of the organization afterwards. There will be a great deal of distress and anger while this process is taking place, both amongst those who are leaving and amongst those who will be staying, who often feel guilty about their 'lucky escape' and whose faith in the organization has been shaken. It may be a good idea to acknowledge this, perhaps using an outside facilitator to maintain the boundaries of the situation and enable people to feel free to express their feelings. Although this may be uncomfortable, it may avoid the creation of simmering resentment and may allow people to progress through the change process we outlined in Chapter 2, moving on to be more positive about the future. This should not be allowed to turn into an ongoing licence to run the organization down, so it is important to maintain the balance between acknowledging people's feelings and colluding with defeatism.

Offering some sort of stress counselling to all employees and career counselling to those who are leaving can help individuals to work in more depth on their personal reactions to the change. It can sometimes be difficult to treat with respect people who are losing their jobs through redundancy, particularly if you feel uncomfortable with the decision or if your own job is under threat, as, by acknowledging them, you may feel that you are weakening your position or indicating that the decision to make the redundancies was a mistake. Those who remain will often judge the organization by the way their departing colleagues are treated, so the way in which the redundancies are handled can have effects far beyond the time limits of the change project. People unsettled by change and guilt have seen the way in which the organization has treated people, and may feel constantly suspicious of the motives of anyone in authority. Thus your handling of the people who are leaving can be as important for the future of the organization as the way you treat the people who will be staying.

Managing the Resistance

Depending on the nature of the change and the cause of the resistance, techniques for managing resistance range along a continuum from the more democratic *involvement* (allowing people to take some part in shaping the change); through *modelling the change* (demonstrating it through your own actions or through showing people models of it actually working elsewhere); *persuasion* (selling the benefits of the change); *negotiation* (examining ways in which you can meet the needs or concerns of those resisting the change in order to reach a compromise); to *using the power of your position to impose the change*. Although it is often better to start at the more democratic end of the continuum and move towards the more autocratic measures only if the resistance persists, this is unwise if the change will involve major restructuring creating a number of losers. In this case, as we have seen, it is better to move the other way along the continuum, dealing with the reorganization first, then inviting those remaining to participate in detailed planning for the way the new organization or service will run.

Typical resistance behaviours

In change situations people often get into stereotyped roles, becoming unable to respond to each situation on its merits. The role definitions shown in Figure 8.2 are often key to understanding people's behaviour (Heron, 1990).

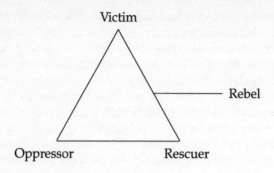

Figure 8.2 *Karpmann drama triangle*

The *oppressor* 'persecutes', or is seen to have 'persecuted', the victim in some way. This may be by making the victim redundant, changing their role, grading or working conditions, or removing some other benefit or protection, or it may be by less of a 'real' event, where the victim feels that they have been injured as a result of action by the oppressor, although the 'oppressor' in fact had little to do with what happened. The oppressor becomes cast as someone who 'has it in for' the victim, and all their actions will then be viewed suspiciously, and motives attributed to them which may be far from their real intention. Even if the 'oppressor' attempts to help the victim in some way, the overture is likely to be rejected or misinterpreted. If you are managing a change project which involves redundancies or other unwelcome changes, you may find that you are cast as the oppressor, with possibly a whole staff group or department as your 'victims'.

The *victim* is helpless in the face of events and the 'aggression' of the oppressor. Again, this may begin as a reaction to events over which the victim genuinely has no control, but it may become a stereotyped role. If the victim's role is changed, meaning that they have to learn and use new skills, they may make no real attempt to learn the skills required, feeling that it is the oppressor's fault that they are in this position and that the oppressor should 'sort things out'. They will not necessarily resist directly, but they may ensure that all attempts to develop them into the new role will fail. This approach may seem very passive, but there is an underlying aggression, a wish to sabotage the oppressor's plans, so the approach is often described as 'passive aggression', because nothing the oppressor does could be right or successful. If, when the victim has failed to adapt to the new role, the oppressor decides to act – by moving the victim again, reducing their level of responsibility or even starting disciplinary proceedings – this will simply confirm the victim's belief that the oppressor is intent on persecuting them.

Once the victim has become identified with the role, they actually need an oppressor. After a number of difficulties or misfortunes it can become easier to take up the position of being helpless rather than to take responsibility for one's own future and decisions. The behaviour of the victim can often become oppressive in itself, aiming to create a constant feeling of guilt in other people. We may all recognize this sort of behaviour, perhaps in our personal as well as our professional lives: the 'martyred' approach to life. This often creates an aggressive response in the oppressor, so the roles become entrenched.

The *rescuer* also responds to the victim's behaviour, by trying to 'save' them. This may be by 'taking their side' against the oppressor, often reducing the possibility of a resolution of the initial difficulties by encouraging the victim to stay in role and continuing to see the oppressor as the cause of all their troubles. Alternatively, the rescuer may intervene by giving the 'helpless' victim a great deal of advice, even making their decisions for them. Again this confirms the victim in their role as helpless and does not encourage them to develop and use their own resources to shape their own lives. In fact, if the victim does try to take a more independent role, the rescuer, far from being pleased, may resist the victim's development, either turning into an oppressor, pouring cold water on all the victim's ideas, or becoming a victim themselves – 'after all I've done for you . . .' – turning the victim into an oppressor. In fact, the rescuer gains self-esteem and maybe even a feeling of power from 'saving' the victim and so they need a victim to save. Thus the triangle of roles becomes self-reinforcing.

The *rebel* appears at first to be different from the other three, standing outside their mutually-reinforcing triangle. In fact the rebel can become just as attached to the role-playing as the others. In some ways the opposite of the victim, the rebel is not truly independent but counter-dependent. This means that he or she will refuse to do things precisely because certain people, usually people in authority, have suggested them. This role is often most clearly seen in adolescence, but may become a pattern in adulthood for some individuals. These people may resist change mainly because it has been suggested by the management, seeing themselves as radical, and therefore persecuted, as they do so. They may also espouse the cause of the 'victim', not to save them but to show that they are prepared to stand up to the management and to make a point. Again, rebels need something or someone to rebel against, and may become victims, oppressors or rescuers in the course of their rebellion. If they were genuinely independent, as they believe, they would consider each event or proposal on its merits, rather than adopting a rebellious stance, often regardless of the actual circumstances.

Not all the behaviours associated with these roles are always inappropriate, of course. If no one was prepared to rebel, there would be few new ideas. Someone in trouble may need assistance from others before they can begin to see their way forward. It is sometimes necessary, particularly in management, to take decisions that you know will disadvantage others and sometimes the only response we can have initially to a devastating event is a feeling of helplessness. It is when these responses to specific situations become roles which will be played out in other, less appropriate, situations that they become damaging.

Guard against collusion

In managing a change project, it is helpful to be aware of these different roles, and to try to guard against being drawn into playing them out. It may be that you have taken a decision which you believe to be necessary although unpopular. If you encounter a 'victim' reaction, you may become irritated, and move from treating a situation on its merits to behaving in an oppressive manner, taking your anger out on the members of your department. You would then be colluding in playing out the victim/oppressor script, turning into an oppressor because that is the role the victim has ascribed to you. This can only lead to worsened organizational relations and a further polarization of positions.

Alternatively, you may start by trying to help members of the department come to terms with the change by presenting it gently, but end up being reluctant to force them to face unpleasant facts and so collude with their denial of the reality of the change. You would unwittingly have slipped into rescuer mode and thereby have deprived them of the opportunity of facing the change and adapting to it.

Perhaps you might start by resisting a change which you genuinely believe would damage the work of your department, but become so vociferous that you cast yourself as a rebel and lose the opportunity to negotiate adjustments to the project to make it less detrimental.

You may find the members of your department are not as supportive of your plans for change as you would wish and respond by making it clear how hurt you are and turning the issue into a personal one, complaining of their 'lack of loyalty' to you. This is likely to lose you their respect, particularly in a time of change when staff will be feeling anxious themselves and will not want to see their manager acting as a helpless victim. In each of these situations you would have slipped into a role which would make it harder for you to see the change clearly and manage any resistance effectively.

So how can you avoid getting caught up in playing out these roles? First, you need to be aware of your predisposition to play certain roles. We all fall into playing one or more of these roles at certain times, generally in times of disagreement or conflict.

CHECKLIST

It can be helpful to reflect on the conflicts or disagreements you have been involved in, particularly those that you were not able to resolve satisfactorily:

- How did you feel and behave at the time?
- Do you recognize any of the roles emerging in the way you handled the conflict?
- Do any of the roles predominate in your memories?

When you know which roles you are most likely slip into, you can watch your behaviour carefully, and stop yourself from getting stuck in role. You may come to recognize that certain behaviour from other people triggers you off, and try to respond to it in a different way. This will prevent the others from being able to remain in their role since, as we saw earlier, the roles depend on each other in order to operate effectively. Thus, if a 'victim' responds assertively and competently, it makes it more difficult for the oppressor to oppress or the rescuer to rescue. If you refuse to respond to passive aggression by 'oppressing', it makes it harder for the 'victim' to maintain their role. Perhaps it would be better to challenge their 'helplessness' by inviting them to help solve the problem. If you refuse to rise to the rebel's challenges and offer to discuss things calmly, it becomes less interesting to rebel and you will not be adding fuel to the fire by your 'unreasonable reaction'.

Challenging inappropriate behaviours

In some circumstances it may be helpful to challenge the behaviour associated with a certain role directly, for example challenging a 'victim's' excuses for inaction, but this must be done carefully and you must be clear that you are not challenging in a way that could add to the role play. For example, 'You're just acting the victim again, like you usually do whenever things get tough!' is accusatory and sounds like the oppressor talking. It is always better to challenge specific behaviour rather than make sweeping statements about the person. The aim of your challenge should be to draw the person's attention to a particular aspect of their behaviour, to explain the effect it is having on you or the project, and to request a change in their behaviour. It is not to score points or make them feel guilty, which is behaviour more likely to come from one of the roles. When deciding whether to challenge, remember that most people play these roles unconsciously, so your challenge may come as a shock. Do not be surprised if some people are unable to take what you say on board immediately. In these circumstances it may be easier just to refuse to play the role they anticipate rather than trying to get them to reflect on their behaviour.

Summary

In this chapter we have reviewed a range of causes of resistance to change and looked at some different ways of managing it. Resistance generally involves conflict of some kind, either direct or more subtle and, as we have seen, this can lead to you losing your clear view of the change project and reacting to events rather than being proactive. It is thus worth continuing to monitor your reaction to resistance to make sure that you are not unnecessarily casting the situation into a battle which one side will win, rather than treating it as a problem which must be solved. It may be helpful to try to ensure that you have access to good support mechanisms when managing change, perhaps including the opportunity to discuss what is happening with someone who is not involved and who can help you to maintain your objectivity. In Chapter 10 we will look further at personal skills and resources available to you. In the next chapter we will look at what happens after the change.

Chapter 9

After the Change

Reviewing and Evaluating the Change Project

As we discussed in Chapter 7, a small change project may have a single transition phase, while a more wide-ranging project may have a number of separate transitions. In the latter case, it may be a good idea to treat each phase as a separate change project and conduct a review of its success, so that any lessons learned can be applied to future phases. The skills of change management are most effectively developed through experience, so it is important to reflect on the projects you have been involved in.

Results of the change for the organization

The first stage is to assess the new situation. Has the organization or department arrived where you thought it would at the beginning of the project? If so, is that destination still appropriate or do you need to reopen the project because other changes have happened around you, making a change of direction necessary?

If the organization or department is not where you thought it would be as a result of the change, is the result of the change acceptable or do you need to reopen the project? Even if the new situation is acceptable, it is helpful to clarify why the end-point of the change is not the one you originally decided on, as this may help you with planning other projects. Did you alter direction part-way through the change project on realizing that your initial aspirations were unrealistic? Have you achieved more than you expected, or found a better way of doing things than you originally planned? Did the political agenda or the demands of the outside world change significantly during the life of the project, making a parallel change of direction inevitable? Was the change process not well monitored so that no one noticed it was drifting off course?

If the change project has not been entirely successful and needs to be reopened, your examination of what has happened may cause you to return to some of the different stages of change management. This may seem laborious, and your first reaction may be to push a bit harder to try to force the change through. This may be appropriate in some circumstances, but there are other occasions when the problem lies in an early stage of the change management process, and forcing tactics will not achieve the desired results. The change may have gone wrong because it was based on an inaccurate diagnosis of the organization's original situation. This could have led to unrealistic goals being set, based on a faulty belief that the organization was sufficiently developed to handle them. Or if the diagnosis was accurate, it may be that the external situation has changed, so that the goals need to be revised. Perhaps the diagnosis and the goals were both appropriate, but the transition was not managed tightly enough, so that the change has gone off course. Finally, it could be that, in directional terms, the change was well planned, but it encountered much greater resistance than expected, making it much more difficult to implement. When you have identified the stage at which the problem originated, you will probably need to reopen the change project from that stage, working through it again to the end.

Review of lessons learned

Even when you are satisfied with the organization's position after the change project, it is helpful to spend some time reviewing the process. You may want to do this on your own, or with the group or department who have been undergoing the change. The following questions may provide a basis for the discussion.

- What lessons can be learned from the project?
- What worked well?
- What worked less well?
- What would you like to have done differently and how will you ensure that this happens next time?
- Are there any development needs for individuals or for the team that emerge from this project and how can these be addressed?

Whether you are answering these questions by yourself or with a team, it is important to remember that the purpose of reviewing the change project is to learn lessons for the future, not to allocate blame or dent your confidence by focusing on areas which did not work perfectly. While it is important to be honest with yourself or with other team members, the aim should be constructive and developmental, not destructive and focused on settling old scores. Also, beware of setting unrealistic standards for yourself. Many change projects are very successful, but we have not found a 'perfect' way of managing change. It will always be possible to find ways in which the project could have been improved, and it is worth knowing about these and acting on them, but it will also always be possible to find aspects that you have done well, and it is good to give yourself credit for these.

Personal review

We each have our own style of change management and the answers to the above questions may tell you something about your style. Which areas of the change project did you find it easiest to work on? Were there any stages which you found very difficult? It may be that you have a very ordered, task-focused style, and that you prefer to work to detailed plans. In that case you will generally manage the transition tightly, but you may fail to take sufficient account of changing circumstances, or of individuals' reactions to the change and you may encounter strong resistance. Or perhaps your general approach is more flexible, so that you can adapt plans as you go along, but you fail to notice that the change is going off course. Each style has some strengths and some weaknesses, and different styles may be appropriate for different situations. In the final chapter we will look more closely at the range of personal skills required for change management, and at how you might develop some of the skills which may be less well developed in your style of change management.

Stabilizing the Change

Once you are satisfied that the changed situation is appropriate for the organization, it is good to let the new status quo 'bed in' for a while; in other words to allow the organization to return to stability with no major changes for a period. As we saw in Chapter 2, change is, by its very nature, destabilizing, and most people would prefer not to be in a situation of constant change. Thus, if another change project emerges quickly you need to ask yourself if it is really crucial to the continuing health and success of the organization. It may be that you have no option other than to introduce the new change, in which case it needs to be planned as carefully as the previous one. It is worth remembering the amount of organizational energy and resources that any major change project will absorb. Change piled upon change almost inevitably means that morale and organizational effectiveness will be reduced, as managers have to spend most of their energy on managing change rather than on managing the service.

It is equally important that the changed situation is maintained during any period of stability following the change project. Sometimes, after a great deal of effort has been put into managing the change, the organization will slip back towards the original status quo after the project has officially ended. People may take short cuts, ignoring the new systems and procedures, or fail to stick to the new service standards. This may be deliberate, or simply an unconscious return to former habits. It must be checked, however, or the change can gradually unravel. Although the change project may be over, you will still have to keep a watchful eye on the progress of the change.

Make sure that you do not revert to any pre-change behaviours as people can take this as a tacit signal that you are not really that concerned about the change and will see it as implied permission for them also to ignore the change. For example, if there is a new structure in the organization, and this has moved the responsibility for a particular task to a new person, support the change by liaising with the new person rather than going back to your old contact, even if this takes longer. Likewise, encourage other members of your team to build the new relationships which will support the change. If a new team has been created, time may need to be devoted to team-building. Further training may need to be given to ensure that people feel fully comfortable with the new skills they are being required to perform. Staff should be encouraged to act in the new ways and, where appropriate, rewarded for doing so. These can be informal rewards, such as praise, or the chance to do interesting work. All these measures help to institutionalize the change.

As the change becomes institutionalized, a certain amount of organizational 'refreezing' will take place. To some extent this is necessary and desirable, as it allows the situation to return to some degree of predictability, and people will become more comfortable. It is also desirable to retain some degree of flexibility, as the environment is unlikely to stay stable for long, and the organization needs to be sufficiently adaptable to cope with this.

The difficulty is to find a way of retaining this flexibility without creating a constant state of turmoil, in other words to balance the sometimes conflicting needs for stability and flexibility. Recently it has been suggested that the concept of the learning organization may be useful in providing a framework for balancing these needs.

The Learning Organization

The learning organization aims to be able to adapt continually to the changing requirements of its environment. It does this by building innovation and flexibility into its day-to-day functioning, rather than by having occasional major change projects. It may use the processes discussed below to do this.

It will have regular work or project reviews to extract learning from practical experience and to plan improvements for the future. The review of the change project mentioned earlier in this chapter is a review of this kind. You could use it to begin a programme of regular reviews within the department or organization.

A learning organization will encourage innovation and creativity amongst the staff. During their work or at the reviews, people will be encouraged to develop new ideas to improve the services or the way in which the organization works. The relaxed, non-evaluative approach that we saw in the visioning chapter will be adopted initially to encourage people to explore the possibilities, followed by a more focused approach to looking at the way the ideas would work in practice. There may be focus groups or multidisciplinary teams brought together to work on particular areas, and staff will be encouraged to liaise across departments. There may be a degree of delegated responsibility to enable people to try out some of their ideas in operation.

A learning organization will encourage and support individual development. This is not solely about encouraging people to go on courses, but more about the attitude of using the work itself to be developmental. Thus, where possible, individuals will be encouraged to take on new responsibilities within their jobs, or perhaps to rotate jobs so that they develop new skills and gain insight into how different procedures or parts of the organization work. This range of perspectives brings innovation to the organization and makes people resourceful and able to cope with operating in different ways in different circumstances.

The organization will review its direction regularly and make sure that it is still following the correct course and meeting the needs of its key stakeholders. It will use this overall direction as a framework for all its activities, the idea being that people can be offered more freedom to innovate in the specific manner in which they do their jobs, provided that they are all working in the same overall direction. Thus the role of management becomes to coordinate and maintain the overall direction and to focus on outcomes, rather than to control specific task performance.

This ideal model is not yet fully operating anywhere in the health service, and there are some conflicts with the more hierarchical management style which operates in some parts of the NHS. Allowing individuals from all parts of the organization to contribute, and possibly act on, their ideas involves a degree of risk. Nevertheless, some elements of the model are applicable. Clinical audit is based on the idea of peer review and of discussing practice to look for improvements. Quality circles are designed to encourage innovation. Many organizations are looking at their approaches to developing their staff and the recent NHS changes have caused most healthcare organizations to review their direction and devise new strategies. Many of the techniques described in this book, including environmental mapping, visioning and using the vision as a basis for overall planning, and reviewing both the outcome and the process of a project, can be used to help create a learning organization. It may be worth exploring whether you want to continue to use any of these techniques with your department or organization after the change project is over, in order to maintain adaptability and flexibility, and perhaps make some future changes gradual evolutions rather than dramatic revolutions.

CHECKLIST

In reviewing your change project, you will need to look at the following areas:

- Has the change project achieved the goals originally set for it?
- If not, do you need to reopen the project and adjust the direction?
- What lessons can be learned from this project? What has gone well and what would you like to do differently in another project?
- How can you support the new teams and relationships which will institutionalize the change?
- How can you ensure that the organization retains some flexibility as the change becomes stabilized?

Summary

In this chapter we have looked at the importance of reinforcing and stabilizing the changed situation, to ensure that the achievements of the change project are maintained. We have also explored how lessons can be learned from this change project, so that the team or organization will be well equipped to face future changes. The change project is now completed. In the final chapter we will return to the personal skills required for managing change and look at how you might develop your understanding of change management further after completing this book.

Chapter 10

Influencing Change

So far we have looked at change management from the perspectives of how individuals and teams typically react to it and in terms of planning for successful change. In this final chapter we will look at how you as an individual manager can maximize the effectiveness of change projects through your own personal and interpersonal behavioural skills. It is obvious but none the less true that, however well formulated and planned change projects may be, they will founder and fail unless the key individuals have the behavioural skills to action them. These skills include the ability to accurately perceive the feelings and reactions of others and to modify behaviour accordingly, while still pursuing clear objectives. They mean acting in clear and uncompromising ways while still treating others with the respect they deserve. They mean role-modelling the espoused values and goals of the organizations in ways that engender commitment and enthusiasm from others. And they mean having a broad and flexible behavioural repertoire which will achieve desired results in a wide variety of situations. Some of these contexts will be individual face-to-face influencing, some will be influencing in team or group settings and some will be organization-wide or public forums.

Managing Oneself

As we have already stated, change will provoke strong reactions in all parts of an organization, at both an individual and a collective level. These reactions will sometimes be irrational and will involve the projection of feelings such as anger and hostility onto those seen as being responsible for the change. As a manager leading change, you will be the recipient of these hostile and angry feelings and you will need the ability to manage your own reactions in an effective way. A common response would be to retaliate and counter such attacks because of the feeling that you are being personally attacked. This is usually a mistake because it tends to precipitate a downward spiral into a win-lose conflict from which there is no escape.

Managing change is inherently stressful because you are dealing with uncertainty, your own and others' future, potential and actual conflict, new tasks, deadlines and almost certainly some level of doubt. Given these pressures and the projection of feelings by others, it is essential that you have some mechanisms for coping and dealing with them. Every individual will have different methods of dealing with pressure, some more effective than others. From experience the positive methods include:

- supervision
- mentoring, and
- learning sets.

Supervision

Supervision should be focused on the change project, allowing you to discuss your experiences and draw out learning from them. Your supervisor needs to have expertise in this area so that they can impart lessons learnt elsewhere, best practice guidelines, etc. Supervision of this sort aims to give some sense of security to you, so that you can review progress in a safe environment and give some expression to the feelings and reactions that are being stirred up within you by the change. If correctly utilized, this sort of input is both supportive and educational; it also helps to protect the organization by ensuring your decisions are well founded. The supervisor is ideally external to your organization but has an understanding of the business.

Mentoring

Mentoring is the practice of having a 'wise elder' within the organization who can act as a personal tutor and guide through the maze of personalities, politics, norms and hidden agendas. In the NHS, mentoring is becoming established as a popular development technique, although usually the mentor is a more senior manager from another hospital rather than from the mentees' own unit. Mentoring skills are being developed so as to provide the 'protégés' with the correct mix of support, guidance and instruction. Mentoring can also be a protective device for change projects since the mentor may have a high degree of clout within the organization.

Learning sets

Joining a learning set for the explicit purpose of gaining support and challenge for particular projects or career periods is also increasingly popular. Here you will be amongst a group of peers from various NHS organizations and will gain the advantages of experiences, insights and learning from a wide variety of perspectives. Facilitated by a set adviser and structured around learning contracts drawn up by each individual, this method is both strongly supportive and powerfully developmental.

In addition to these there are a variety of formal and informal support and development techniques that individuals can avail themselves of, including discussing issues and problems with colleagues, peers or friends; going on external training and development courses; or switching attention and energy by engaging in sporting, recreational or social activities.

Whatever the method or technique, the important point is that when managing change you make available time and opportunity to examine the personal impacts and how you are managing them.

Influencing Others

In order to influence others in a positive way, managers need effective interpersonal skills that are sensitive to the particular individuals involved. These skills can be categorized under two headings: the facilitative and the directive. The former includes skills which are used to draw other people out, to explore others' positions and areas of salient common experience and common ground. These skills include the following:

- *Active learning* – this is the ability to practise accurate listening and understanding of others' statements and positions. It includes subsidiary skills such as summarizing, paraphrasing and reflecting.
- *Exploration* – using open and closed questions in ways that help to explore and refine understanding both for oneself and others.
- *Self-disclosure* – appropriate use of one's own experience or values can help to illuminate similarities or build bridges between people and demonstrates both understanding and integrity if deployed effectively.
- *Dealing with feelings* – the ability to enable others to manage their feelings more effectively is a subtle but powerful one. It may be deployed in tacit ways by allowing people to express how they feel about issues, or it may be more explicit as in encouraging others to look beneath the expression of conflict to the feelings and anxieties that fuel it.

On the directive side, the skills are used to shape others' perceptions and expectations, to challenge and confront others' viewpoints, to provide a rationale, data and meaning and to spell out negative and positive consequences of actions. The skills that are important to achieve these ends are:

- *Challenge* – the ability to confront opposing views or positions in a constructive way is a difficult but crucial one. During change situations it is vital that boundaries and parameters are vigorously upheld; only by challenging and confronting their transgression in clear but uncompromising ways is this possible. Spelling out the consequences of disagreement or inaction may be necessary.
- *Stating one's own position* – the ability to articulate the change required and the rationale behind it with clarity, focus and insistence. This will include the marshalling of logic, data and

information as well as the subjective expression of one's own views and opinions.

- *Prescribing action* – the skill of stating the action required from people in clear behavioural terms with attached timescales is obviously important. This means spelling out areas of responsibility and accountability and gaining agreements from others.
- *Painting the future picture* – this lies somewhere between self-disclosure and stating your own position. It is the skill of generating enthusiasm and motivation for the vision that lies at the heart of the change being undertaken. Much of the skill relies on the general ability to build up credibility with others, but it takes this further by using persuasion emanating from a clear belief in what you are doing and an excitement for the possibilities. It goes without saying that you yourself must be convinced by the change and believe in the way forward.

These skills will not necessarily be present or may be under-utilized, usually for one of the following three reasons:

1. A lack of knowledge about the range of possible behaviours for influencing.
2. A lack of practice utilizing these skills.
3. Knowledge and practice are present but something blocks the application or deployment of them, for instance
   - psychological blocks ('I can't be assertive', etc.)
   - cultural constraints (norms and agendas within the organization)
   - gender barriers (men/women don't behave like that).

As a manager you need to be clear about the effectiveness of your influencing skills and the weaknesses that may hamper you. There are a number of ways of achieving this: one would be to gather work-based feedback from people who have a knowledge of your working life. There are a number of questionnaires which can help to structure or formalize this process; they may help to make the feedback anonymous and so safer for others to be honest. Another method is to go on an external development course; a number of these exist looking at areas like personal power, influencing skills or assertiveness. Many will make use of video-based feedback and role play which can be very helpful in exploring the important non-verbal elements of communication. Alternatively, you may use forums such as supervision to identify particular pieces of managerial practice for more intensive review. Again, as in managing oneself, it is vital that influencing others is a reflective practice and that you take the time to explicitly develop your skills and abilities.

Managing Groups

A lot of change management takes place in group settings, such as dedicated project groups (set up to project manage the change), clinical teams, ward teams, management groups, executive boards, etc.

It can be very useful to understand something of the way groups work and the potential dysfunctional aspects of groups. It is also crucial to be able to deploy the behavioural skills necessary to facilitate groups as these are not always the same as influencing on an individual basis.

A useful model of group development is Tuckman's 'group life' (1965). He postulates five main stages in the life of a group:

- forming
- storming
- norming
- performing, and
- mourning.

At each stage the leader of the group may need to exercise different skills and play a different role.

Stage I: forming

In the early stages of a group the issues for members concern orientation and inclusion: 'Do I belong here?', 'What is expected of me?' There is a natural anxiety and uncertainty which must be managed by the leader. In this stage the leader must vigorously clarify the group's task and ensure that the membership of the group is established and that people feel as though they have a role or part to play. The establishment of clear ground rules and/

or terms of reference is one way of establishing clear boundaries and expectations.

Stage 2: storming

Once a certain level of confidence and inclusion is established, the group will move on to explore and test out power and authority. This will usually be directed at the leader and will involve questioning of their decisions and maybe challenge or confrontation. It is vital that the leader holds firm at this stage, while becoming neither too aggressive nor too wounded. Some of the questioning may be legitimate, and it is important that group members feel that the leader is strong yet reasonable.

Stage 3: norming

Once issues of power and authority have been clarified, the group will get down to looking at the systems, processes and structures by which the task will be achieved. The leader's role becomes less directive and more facilitative, providing structures for members and ensuring that individuals' strengths are utilized and contributions maximized. There may need to be a challenge to hidden agendas or group norms which become insidiously established or which are imported into the group from the organization. These will be unquestioned assumptions about things like hierarchy, decision making, professional roles, etc. If left unchallenged, these things can make a group either uncreative or actively dysfunctional.

Stage 4: performing

This is the production phase of the task. The group's energy is high, there is a sense of synergy and collective effort, people are clear about what they need to do and are getting on with it. The leader's task is to monitor and steer the group, to ensure that external communication is maintained and to pass the leadership role over to others for certain tasks or phases. It is important that the group identity does not get so strong at this stage that it separates itself off from the rest of the organization. The leader needs to maintain permeable boundaries and to ensure that the change activities are being taken out into the wider organization.

Stage 5: mourning

Having done its work, the group may disband or move on to other tasks. It is important to ensure that this is done clearly and explicitly. It can be useful to have a celebratory ritual to mark the end of a piece of work, such as a meal or a party where the collective effort that has been put in is recognized by all concerned. The leader's task is to ensure that the ending happens clearly, that learning from the project is drawn out and taken back into the organization and that any unfinished business is dealt with or let go of.

The sort of skills that are important in leading groups include being able to establish a climate of trust and safety, often through establishing group rules and ensuring that people feel valued. The facilitator must have the ability to set clear goals and direction and then to ensure that the task remains in focus at all times. They must be sensitive to individuals' feelings and the collective group mood and, if necessary, work on them before addressing the task. They must be able to confront individuals' hidden agendas and group norms in ways that are challenging but supportive and they must be able to provide frameworks of meaning for what is happening and have the ability to structure the group's activities so that it achieves its tasks.

Learning these things is usually a matter of experience; over the years you gain exposure to a wide variety of groups and build up mechanisms for managing and coping with them. A repertoire of skills is built up that works in most settings most of the time. However it may be necessary to reflect on the way you lead groups and the repertoire of skills you possess. You can get feedback from one or two trusted people who are members of groups that you lead, you can use supervision, mentoring or learning sets to review case examples or critical incidents, or you can pursue external courses in leadership and facilitation. Whatever the method, it is advisable to review and refresh skills continuously as change requires continual renewal and updating.

CHECKLIST

1. Make a list of all the means by which you gain support for your work.
   - What is the balance of these activities in terms of formal mechanisms like supervision and informal processes like leisure and recreation?
   - Do you feel that you are getting the right quality and quantity of support to help you do your job effectively?
   - What other support resources are available that you are currently not utilizing?
   - What other support resources need to be created to meet your support needs?

2. List the ways in which you provide support for the staff in your team or department.
   - How do you determine the level and type of support that staff need to help them through the change situation?
   - Are you meeting the genuine support needs of your staff?
   - What more do you need to do to meet these needs?

3. Reflect on the ways in which you have tried to influence key people to accept the changes you are trying to achieve.
   - Would you characterize your influencing style as predominantly facilitative or directive?
   - Which specific influencing skills do you tend to use in most situations and is this intentional or unconscious?
   - Which skills do you rarely or never use and why is this (lack of practice, psychological blocks, etc)?
   - What development needs do you have in terms of influencing and what are the ways in which you could meet these (training courses, peer feedback, etc)?

4. Analyse the way in which you are using group settings to achieve change.
   - What is your predominant style of leading groups: facilitative or directive?
   - Are the groups you are in stuck at certain stages (forming and storming, for instance) and what can you do to achieve effective movement through the early stages?

> - How do the groups you are in go about problem solving, decision making and conflict resolution?
> - What development needs do you have in terms of leading groups and how might you meet these needs?

Case Study

A development programme to increase influencing ability

The managers of an Acute Trust that we were working with wanted to increase the organization's readiness and capability to manage change, particularly in terms of utilizing areas of work important to the new NHS such as business management, clinical leadership, marketing, information technology and quality. It especially wanted to use people with this expertise in more of an internal consultancy role so that their influence and knowledge were spread across the organization. To achieve this aim we put together a change management programme targeted at a cross-section of key individuals with responsibilities in these areas.

The programme consisted of three linked modules with project-based work in between the modules to provide real data for reflection, feedback, planning and rehearsal. The first of these modules was very much focused on the individual and their interpersonal management style. Prior to the module itself, participants gathered structured feedback from work colleagues (peers, those they managed and those that managed them) about their influencing style and skills. They then utilized this feedback plus videoed role plays and group simulations to build up profiles of their influencing ability and the development needs that they had. These needs were then practised in videoed role play exercises based on real work situations, with much emphasis on self- and peer feedback and review to facilitate learning.

Between the first and second module, participants attempted to put learning goals into practice in real-life influencing situations and brought the results back for review.

The second module consisted of developing consultancy skills and building effective business relationships with both internal and external customers. As part of this module, outside managers took part in a business simulation designed to demonstrate the key issues in becoming effective in these key areas. Again there was a strong emphasis on self- and peer feedback as a learning device. Between the second and third modules, participants put identified learning goals into practice and brought these back to the third module for review.

The third module consisted of a workshop format utilizing participants' real work-based change projects and applying some of the change management techniques that have been covered in this book. By the end of the module, participants had identified likely sources and causes of resistance and come up with strategies to overcome them, had developed long-term goals and short-term milestones, and had identified key project management roles and responsibilities. Between the third module and a final follow-up day some months later, participants put their change projects into operation and brought the results back for review.

The final day was also used to assimilate learning from the whole programme and to look at participants' further development needs. As a result of this a number of informal learning sets were established (which continued to meet over the following months) designed to provide both support and a learning environment for the members while they pursued their various change projects.

Programme to develop group facilitation skills

A Community Trust we worked with wished to develop group facilitation skills with the aim of producing a pool of facilitators across the organization who would set up and run quality monitoring groups as part of the Trust's overall quality management programme. This style of running groups was also an attempt to change the culture of the organization from a centrally-driven and predominantly hierarchical model to a more locally-determined and team-based form of service delivery working much more closely with GP practices.

The facilitators would have responsibility for both introducing change in natural work groups and for feeding back to a board-level quality assurance group on significant quality issues affecting patient care. Facilitators would also have the task of identifying and developing successive facilitators so that there was a continual replenishment of talent and enthusiasm.

The development programme was divided into a conceptual theme and a practical theme. The former involved inputs on areas like stages of group development, facilitation tasks at these different stages, defence mechanisms in groups and styles and skills of group facilitation in different contexts. The latter theme involved participants identifying their own facilitation style using group exercises with peer feedback, and critical incident analysis where participants looked at how they had dealt with difficult and demanding situations in group settings.

From this participants identified their strengths and their development needs, designed group exercises to gain practice for the latter and looked at how they would apply the learning in their own quality groups.

There was then a break of a couple of months to allow participants to apply the lessons to the actual groups they facilitated. There was a follow-up module where the facilitation experiences were reviewed and learning shared, where individual development goals were assessed and adjusted as necessary and where further learning opportunities were identified.

Summary

In this final chapter we have looked at some of the individual behavioural skills and abilities that will mediate the success or otherwise of change projects, particularly the ability to manage oneself, to influence individuals and to manage/facilitate groups. We have stressed the importance of developing and reviewing these skills in a continuous way and of ensuring that you have personal support mechanisms set up to deal with the differing reactions and impact of change. It is vital that you, the individual manager as the main instrument of change, do not forget to pay attention to the most important determiner of change – yourself.

Further Reading

Argyris, C (1990) *Overcoming Organisational Defenses*, Allyn and Bacon.

Beckhard, R (1969) *Organisation Development: strategies and models*, London: Addison-Wesley.

Beckhard, R and Harris, R (1987) *Organisational Transitions*, London: Addison-Wesley.

Boss, R (1989) *Organisation Development in Health Care*, London: Addison-Wesley.

Brown, R (1988) *Group Processes*, Oxford: Blackwell.

Daniel Duck, J (1993) 'Managing change: the art of balancing', *Harvard Business Review*, Nov–Dec 1993.

Drucker, P (1992) *Managing The Non-Profit Organisation*, London: Butterworth-Heinemann.

Galbraith, J (1973) *Designing Complex Organisations*, London: Addison-Wesley.

Handy, C (1985) *Understanding Organisations*, Harmondsworth: Penguin.

Harrison, S, Hunter, D and Pollitt, C (1990) *The Dynamics of British Health Policy*, London: Unwin Hyman.

Heron, J (1989) *The Facilitator's Handbook*, London: Kogan Page.

Heron, J (1990) *Helping the Client*, London: Sage.

Holdaway, K and Saunders, M (1992) *The In-House Trainer as Consultant*, London: Kogan Page.

Kolb DA, Rubin IM and McIntyre JM (1974) *Organisational Psychology: An experiential approach*, Hemel Hempstead: Prentice-Hall.

Kubler-Ross, E (1969) *On Death and Dying*, London: Macmillan.

Lewin, K (1965) 'Group decisions and social change' in Proshansky, H and Seidenberg, B (Eds) *Basic Studies in Social Psychology*, London: Holt, Rinehart and Winston.

Schein, E (ed.) (1987) *The Art of Managing Human Resources*, Oxford: Oxford University Press.

Schein, E (1980) *Organisational Psychology*, Hemel Hempstead, Prentice-Hall.

Tuckman, BW (1965) 'Developmental Sequence in Small Groups', *Psychological Bulletin*.

Index